NOBODY GETS RICH WORKING

NOBODY GETS RICH WORKING FOR SOMEBODY ELSE

THE ESSENTIAL GUIDE FOR EVERY ENTREPRENEUR

Roger Fritz

Foreword by Ted Fuller,
Deputy Director of Durham University
Business School

THORSONS PUBLISHING GROUP

First published 1987 by Dodd, Mead and Company, Inc., 79 Madison
Avenue, New York, N.Y. 10016.
This UK edition published 1989.
Copyright © Roger Fritz.

The Snake That Poisons Everybody, copyright © 1981 United Technologies.
Reprinted with the permission of United Technologies.

Editor's note
This book is intended as an inspirational overview to business for the
small businessperson. It is *not* a complete handbook to running a business
and should not be treated as such. Any reader considering going into
business is encouraged to obtain professional advice and counselling.
The UK case studies I have introduced into the book are all known to
me personally and my thanks are extended to the entrepreneurs for their
permission to publish these cases.

Ted Fuller

British Library Cataloguing in Publication Data

Fritz, Roger
Nobody gets rich working for somebody else.
— UK ed.
1. Small firms. Organisation, — Manuals
I. Title
658'.022

ISBN 0-7225-1615-0

Published by Thorsons Publishing Group, Wellingborough,
Northamptonshire, NN8 2RQ, England

Printed in Great Britain by Billing & Sons Limited, Worcester
Typeset by MJL Limited, Hitchin, Hertfordshire

1 3 5 7 9 10 8 6 4 2

Contents

To my mother and father, who were never rich but nevertheless had a priceless gift to give — their undying confidence in me!

To every man and woman who has started a new venture and survived. Whatever good this book may do is a tribute to you — all of you!

Foreword
by Ted Fuller
Deputy Director of Durham University
Business School

There has never been a better time to start your own enterprise. Access to technology, the improvements in communications and the wider opportunities in Europe are just some of the positive environmental factors. Socially and politically, small is beautiful and enterprise is an esteemed personal quality. The cultural heroes of this generation include such entrepreneurs as Richard Branson, Sir Terence Conran and Rupert Murdoch.

More people are starting their own small business. The number of self-employed people has increased by about 20 per cent over the past five years. At least 100,000 new businesses are started each year. Small business accounts for most of new jobs over the past five years too.

For those who have the right attitude, the world is full of opportunities to take. People have needs to be met; inefficiencies exist which could be improved on; poorly performing products can be replaced by innovations. All you have to do is take the opportunities which are under your own nose.

For many people with the urge to do something for themselves, starting their own business represents a completely different way of life, with new rules to learn. New enterprises can and do fail sometimes.

Obviously, the better prepared one is to undertake the creation and operation of a new business venture, the more likely the chances of success are. That is the purpose of this book. As the author himself says in his introduction to the US edition, the book is to help you gain a better understanding of your own business capabilities, of the process of running a successful business, of the value of developing strong individual leadership skills, of the ways to attract and retain good employees and of the techniques for guiding the business as it grows.

We wish you every success.

Preface

This book has been more than a writing project. It has been a mission — a total immersion — in recalling, researching, and recording what it takes to start, maintain, and grow a business venture. Because the failure rate is so very, very high, I wanted to have available in one volume a source to which anyone could quickly and easily turn for thorough, useful, and accurate information. In other words, I firmly believe that the success rate can be improved significantly. If this book contributes to that improvement, my objective will be achieved.

Acknowledgement

The other key person engaged in this project has been Don Young. His insights, experience, and skills have been involved throughout. My greatest hope is that he will now enjoy a well-earned retirement in sunny Arizona.

Introduction

Until the middle of the nineteenth century people followed the came career paths as their parents. Girls, of course, stayed home and learned to cook, sew, and keep house until they got married and became wives and mothers. Boys traditionally followed in the footsteps of their fathers. If the father were a farmer, as most fathers were, the son also became a farmer; if the father were a printer or a blacksmith or a merchant, the son became a printer or a blacksmith or a merchant.

However, things changed considerably with Industrialization. It brought increased opportunity and eliminated many types of work entirely. It resulted in the development of large corporations and large cities. It provided us with fast, reliable, inexpensive transportation — first the train, then the car, and eventually the airplane — that enabled us to pursue careers whenever and wherever an opportunity existed. And it caused us to become more aware of education and of its value to those who seek a more satisfying way of life.

Now, equally dramatic changes are taking place. Many major industries, such as automobiles and steel, are have serious difficulties in their battle against foreign competition. New technologies, from frozen foods to microcomputers, are altering not only our lifestyles but the manner in which we do business. The average American — both male and female — has a higher level of education than ever before. Women now are involved in virtually every field of endeavour and constitute over 43 percent of our entire workforce. Over 46 percent of all American households include a working husband *and* a working wife. Four million Americans (half of them white-collar professionals) now hold two jobs. Those who are not educationally prepared are more and more out of step with the job market and the economic opportunities that exist. Workers no longer are content to live in the congested 'work centres' of the past, and many regions, such as Detroit and Gary, Indiana, are deteriorating rapidly. Today, the action is shifting to the Sun Belt. As a result of their ever increasing demands for more pay, increased fringe benefits, less productivity, and greater authority within the industries in which they work, the nation's unions have virtually stifled both corporate and individual progress in a number of the largest and most critical industries.

In addition, many Americans of all ages, of both sexes, in every geographic region, are growing disenchanted with traditional corporate work habits and are seeking alternative means of employment. Many of them are are creating businesses of their own.

According to David Birch, a professor at the Massachusetts Institute of Technology, two-thirds of all new jobs created between 1969 and 1976 were in firms with fewer than twenty employees. Companies with fewer than 250 personnel now employ 70 per cent of our total workforce. No fewer than half a million new companies are formed each year in America.

Is this good or bad for the United States?

In the early 1920s, W. Clement Stone invested $100 to start a business of his own. Today, Combined Insurance Company of America is a multibillion-dollar firm that provides employment for 14,500 people.

In 1965, Joe Hrudka founded Mr. Gasket Company with an outlay of five dollars. In 1969, he took the company public. In 1971, he sold Mr. Gasket to W. R. Grace & Company for $17 million. In 1981, he bought the company back for $4 million. And in 1983, he took the company public again, earning himself a personal fortune of $87 million on the offering.

In 1978, a Cuban who had escaped the Castro regime, Joel Newman, and two refugee friends put up $20,000 to start Cosmo Communications Corporation. Cosmo grew to become the world's largest manufacturer of digital clocks, and in 1983, the company went public. Newman's personal stock in the firm at the time of the offering was valued at $44 million.

In spite of these outstanding success stories, it should be remembered that starting a business is a gamble and, like any gamble, involves the opportunity to fail as well as the opportunity to succeed. An individual may excel in his or her own field of specialization, but that is no guarantee that he/she will be successful in business.

Obviously, the better prepared one is to undertake the creation and operation of a new business venture, the more likely the chances of success are. That is the purpose of this book: to help you gain a better understanding of your own business capabilities, of the process of running a successful business, of the value of developing strong individual leadership skills, of the ways to attract and retain good employees, and of the techniques for guiding the business as it grows.

We wish you every success.

Part I

Your own business

1
Could *you* be an entrepreneur?

Actually, it's not all that bad to work for somebody else.

In most cases it means steady work with a regular income and perhaps a periodic bonus or raise. You probably get the usual fringe benefits — paid holidays, life and medical insurance, and so on — and you may even participate in profit sharing, share options, and other economically attractive incentive plans.

If the work runs out, it's usually somebody elses responsibility to bring in more. If the work piles up, there's usually someone available to help you. If you get sick, there's probably someone who can fill in for you. If you make a big mistake the most you can lose is your job.

Many companies will also finance part or all of your tuition if you wish to continue your education.

Depending on your line of work, you may have the use of a company car or the opportunity to travel to Tokyo, Paris, New York or anywhere in the world, all at company expense. If it's a large company with a number of factory or office locations, you may even have considerable flexibility in determining where you'd like to live.

You probably have a rather clear-cut career path, readily discernible if you study your chain of command. After a satisfying career you will be able to enjoy a reasonably comfortable retirement through the company pension plan. These are all factors worth consideration. Some people tend to forget them unless they are reminded. Why, then, would anyone want to abandon all that and venture out alone into a brand-new business?

The benefits of being the boss

It is well known that, in Britain, nearly 40 per cent of firms fail within the first three years. In the USA the failure rate is even higher, which is not evidence of poor management, but that more people try it for themselves. Against these bleak statistics, why do so many people find self-employment so attractive?

Control of your own destiny

Many individuals find 'regular' employment dissatisfying because it forces them to accept conditions of someone else's choosing. They may not like the people with whom they work, the geographic location of the office, the prescribed work hours, the general working conditions, the assigned responsibilities outside their own area of interest, the possibilities for advancement, or the lack of opportunity to try something new and different. The company may be poorly managed or in bad financial condition, there may be frequent lay-offs, or perhaps the firm is family operated, allowing little hope of growth or promotion to an outsider.

Being the boss allows you more independence and more control over your own destiny.

Satisfying the creative urge

If an individual has *truly* designed a better mousetrap — or discovered a better way to *sell* the mousetrap — or devised a way to cure the common cold, starting a new business may be the simplest, most direct, fastest, and most satisfying way to take the idea to the public. In any event, there is a great deal of personal gratification in being able to say, 'I did it my way!'

Numerous studies have shown that smaller companies are more creative, more productive, and more responsive to changing conditions in the market-place than are their larger counterparts. To become a part of this life in the fast lane can be intellectually and physically stimulating. It can provide fulfilment for those who wish to demonstrate their usefulness and their accomplishment.

Starting a business of your own can give you personal, social, economic, and professional status. It can satisfy the demands of your ego, and it can validate your worth.

The financial rewards

Obviously, the potential for financial reward is greater for a boss than for an employee. The one who takes the most risk, who is willing to gamble money, time, talent, and reputation, and who shoulders the heaviest responsibility for the success — or failure — of the enterprise is entitled to the greatest reward.

Apart from the salary that the boss takes out of the business, there are other financial rewards as well. As the business prospers and is able to provide a greater number of perks, the boss can retain more of his or her personal income. As the business grows, so, too, does the value of the boss's equity. And the more equity the boss controls, when and if the company should decide to go public or merge with another firm, the greater the boss's share of the proceeds.

Our tax laws are structured to aid the risk-takers. Many expenses are tax-deductible if you are running a business. If the firm is incorporated, the profits are taxed at a lower rate than personal income is. And, if you eventually sell the company — or sell some of your shares in the company — you may pay taxes on the capital gain at a much more favourable rate.

These benefits only accrue if your business is successful and profitable, of course. Whether that occurs will depend very strongly on your ability to start and maintain the company, recruit good staff and guide the firm on a path toward future growth and prosperity.

The greatest rewards often go to those who take the greatest risks: Thomas Edison pioneered in the field of electricity, Henry Ford pioneered the concept of mass production. But, just in case you let their success cloud your judgement, remember the definition of a *pioneer* — he's the one with the arrows in his back!

Almost all new companies begin as viable, worthwhile ventures. Some even make a profit during their first few months of operation. But the ones that last are the ones that have knowledgeable leadership, a plan for the future, and a strong commitment to succeed.

One should never start a business with the idea that, 'I'll try it for a year or two.' That attitude is seldom sufficient to get a business started, guide it over the rough spots, and lead it firmly toward future growth and success.

Lee Iacocca, the head of Chrysler Corporation, has often been asked, 'After you joined Chrysler and discovered how much trouble the company was in, didn't you consider throwing in the towel?' Iacocca's answer, 'Never. *Once I'd made the commitment,* I never lost my determination to do everything that I could to make the company successful.'*

That is the commitment that saved Chrysler — and the commitment that any entrepreneur needs in order to start and develop a successful company.

The personality of an entrepreneur

Successful businesses are formed by people who share a number of important personality characteristics. A successful entrepreneur must

- Have a capacity for work — including a willingness to put in long hours.
- Be goal-orientated.
- Be a self-starter who doesn't need to be 'pushed.'
- Have good judgement.
- Be self-confident, but not egotistical.
- Be honest.
- Be persistent.
- Be a problem-solver — every problem is a new challenge and a new opportunity.
- Have the capability to take a risk.
- Be people-orientated.
- Be profit-orientated.
- Have flexibility and adaptability.
- Have accountability.
- Have a desire to win.
- Be innovative.

*Reprinted with permission of the author, Bonnie Remsburg, *Success* magazine (January 1982).

Test your own potential

On a scale of one to ten (lowest to highest), evaluate yourself as to these entrepreneurial characteristics.

Capacity for work ___8___   7
Goal-orientated ___9___   9
A self-starter ___8___   8
Good judgement ___8___   8
Self-confident ___8___   7
Honest ___10___   10
Persistent ___10___   10
A problem-solver ___8___   7
Capability to take a risk ___10___   9
People-orientated ___15___   4
Profit-orientated ___7___   5
Flexibility and adaptibility ___9___   9
Accountability ___9___   9
Desire to win ___9___   6
Innovative ___9___   8

Total ___132___   121

The value of this rating depends on the answer you gave to one characteristic — honesty. If you haven't been totally honest with yourself in evaluating all these factors, then the results will have to be adjusted accordingly. It is wiser to evaluate yourself too low than too high.

If your score was between 120 and 150, you have a strong entrepreneurial personality and will probably do very well as the boss of a new business.

If you scored between 100 and 120, you probably have enough of the right stuff to be successful if you make the effort to bolster your skills in the weaker areas.

If you scored between 80 and 100, you probably should not try to shoulder a new business on your own. Look for partners or reliable employees who can strengthen the firm in the areas where you are weak.

If you scored less than 80, you will probably be happier and more successful as a manager in someone else's company than in a business of your own.

What about brains?

Perhaps you've noticed that genius is not one of the characteristics commonly found in successful entrepreneurs. Al McGuire, the brilliant American basketball-coach-turned-sportscaster, has observed that 'the world is run by C students'. Many others have made the same observation.

Street sense is much more valuable to a businessman than academic intelligence. No college or university, at this point in time, awards an MBE — Master's in Business Entrepreneurship — although it should be noted that a number of institutions are beginning to add entrepreneurship to their curricula. Over 2,500 secondary schools in Britain run practical 'enterprise' classes. Enterprise training is a requirement within the curriculum of Youth Training Schemes and Employment Training. Many colleges of higher and further education include enterprise in the curriculum. Stirling University offers a Masters degree in enterprise studies and Durham University offers a Diploma in Enterprise Management for young graduates working as managers in small firms. Half a dozen universities and polytechnics train young graduates to start businesses and over 1,500 graduates take three-month projects in small firms to get a 'taste' of entrepreneurship. The 1990s will herald 'enterprise' as competence in the way that marketing, accountancy or information technology are heralded today.

Obviously, the head of a company must have a thorough knowledge of the field in which he or she works, whether it's motor mechanics or aerospace, but success as a leader will depend on a number of far less objective things.

Are you an individual performer or a team worker?

Individual performers make great employees, but they seldom make good bosses. The boss must realize that one cannot do everything alone; that a well-rounded and efficient team has to be formed; and that, if the team is to function properly, a great many duties and responsibilities have to be delegated to other people. Even if the boss is the strongest individual performer on the team, she still is only one part of the team.

An effective leader knows that one cannot continually second-guess the employees or put too many restrictions on their freedom. When this happens, they will become too absorbed in the *process* of doing their work, rather than the *reason* for doing it, and — even worse — they will be afraid to try something new, to do something different, or to take a gamble. This attitude leads to stagnation, not growth.

Have you taken charge of yourself?

Have you taken the time to analyse yourself — to understand what makes you tick? Are you consistent? Are you methodical? Are you well organized? Do you understand — and can you cope with — your weaknesses as well as your strengths?

If you have not learned to control your own life, you will have a great many difficulties dealing with the problems of a business — and its employees — as well. Unless you have developed a degree of consistency, for example, you may discover that you're constantly sending out confusing signals to your employees, and that they are spending more time trying to cope with the boss than they are spending on productive effort.

Have you developed a core of confidence?

Confidence is not cockiness, and it is not stubbornness. It is simply calm self-assurance.

Good leaders must have confidence. They must be able to make decisions and avoid both procrastination (delay in making a decision) and vacillation (waffling on a decision). Those who vacillate will demonstrate that they are uncertain, thereby weakening the effect of the decision and inviting those who do not agree with it to either argue with it or ignore it.

Do you have the power of purpose?

Are you goal-orientated? Have you set your sights on an objective and committed yourself to reaching it?

The shortest distance between two points is a straight line, and your company will stand a greater chance of success if there is a strong hand on the tiller.

As the boss, you must set the goals — but they must be realistic, attainable goals. (See Chapter 9.)

If your motivation for going into business is to enable yourself to sleep late in the morning, you'll probably be disappointed. Entrepreneurs often work 10 to 16 hours a day.

If your motivation is quick financial gain, you'll probably still be disappointed. During the early stages of developing a business, the boss often makes less than the employees.

Your purpose must be consistent with the success of the business, and your commitment must be stronger than that of your strongest employee if you are to become a successful businessperson.

Do you have self-discipline?

When you work for someone else, you're told what time to be in the office, what days to work, what results are expected of you, with whom to work, what to do, how to do it, when to do it, and much, much more. When you run your own business, *you* must make all of those decisions — not only for yourself, but for your employees as well.

Are you flexible?

Like uncharted reefs in the water, a number of obstacles can stand in the way between your company and its goals. The cost of labour or materials may go up. A competitor may introduce a new product. One of your key people may resign. A major supplier may go bankrupt. You may lose your principal customer. If the strong hand on the tiller cannot steer the ship around these reefs, the company may go aground.

While continuing to keep an eye on the ultimate goal, a boss must be flexible enough to make adjustments in the company as necessary. One choice may be safer, but may take longer or be more expensive. Another may be less costly or faster, but riskier. It is up to the skipper to make the decisions.

What about family?

Few people set out to conquer the world alone. Almost everyone needs a support group of some kind. For most of us, that group is our family.

The family that provides us with strength and encouragement may be a marital family (spouse, children), a parental family (father, mother), a sibling family (brother, sister), or some other family of friends and relatives. Whatever its nature, we rely on this family more heavily than most of us realize, and its support can be absolutely crucial to someone starting a new business.

Typically, the individual who starts a business will suffer a great deal of insecurity, fear, anxiety, and hesitancy — at least until the business is established and operating smoothly. Your family, through its loyalty and its often unquestioning confidence in you, will help you over those hurdles.

Typically, orders won't come in as quickly as you'd like; customers won't pay their bills on time, you won't be able to find suitable help, a key piece of equipment may break down. The family is sympathetic — and may even pitch in to help.

Typically, an entrepreneur will work long hours, forgo salary if finances are tight, skip a long-anticipated holiday. The family understands.

Occasionally, in spite of everything that can be done, a business will fail and the entrepreneur will lose everything that has been invested in it. A sensitive family will accept that without recrimination and will tell you, 'At least you gave it your best shot.'

Are you saying at this point, 'Oh, no they won't! Not *my* family!'? If so, perhaps you should give more thought to the idea of starting a business.

Nothing undermines personal relationships as much as tension. This is true of friends, of neighbours, or relatives — and especially of marriages. Starting a business produces a lot of tension. Can your marriage take it? You'd better be sure.

Bitter fights, separations, divorces, and, in extreme cases, even murders have resulted from the type of stress that is, if not common, at least not unusual in starting a business. Spouses no longer spend as much time together as before. Parents no longer have as much time for their children. The income, even when it is adequate (which, on occasion, it may not be), is not steady and dependable. Promises are made and then, because of the business, broken. Money that once would have been spent on presents, on vacations, or on dinners out may now go into the business. The harried entrepreneur, burdened with business problems, may just not be any fun anymore.

Do you have a strong marriage? Are you absolutely sure? Going into business could be a tragic way of discovering that you're wrong.

Which is the most important — the business or the marriage? Some people have ended up losing both!

The following quiz obviously can do no more than serve as a guide, but, even as that, it may prove very revealing and helpful.

See how *you* think your *spouse* would answer the following questions.

Your spouse is attempting to start a new business. As a result, a number of situations (listed below) have come about. Express your feelings as honestly as you possibly can and indicate whether in each of these situations, were it to happen to you, you would be strongly displeased, you would be displeased, or you would understand.

	Strongly displeased	Displeased	Would understand
1 *After ten years of economizing to save £20,000 your spouse withdraws the entire amount to invest in a business.*	_____	_____	_____
2 *Twice in the past week, dinner was delayed for more than an hour because your spouse didn't get home.*	_____	_____	_____

	Strongly displeased	Displeased	Would understand
3 Something you badly wanted to buy was placed on hold because all available cash was needed for the business.	_____	_____	_____
4 Your spouse gives up fifteen years of seniority with the company to go into business now.	_____	_____	_____
5 Your spouse promises to go to the theatre with you and then has to back out.	_____	_____	_____
6 You forfeit all your present pension rights.	_____	_____	_____
7 Your spouse promises to go to the zoo with the children but then has to back out.	_____	_____	_____
8 You are no longer covered by free medical and dental insurance.	_____	_____	_____
9 Your parents are in town for a visit, but your spouse is away on business.	_____	_____	_____
10 You have to move to another town.	_____	_____	_____
11 Because a client delays paying a bill, your spouse has to borrow from the bank to meet expenses.	_____	_____	_____
12 Your spouse has to do a lot of night work.	_____	_____	_____
13 The business needs a new piece of equipment, so your spouse takes out a second mortgage on the house.	_____	_____	_____

	Strongly displeased	Displeased	Would understand
14 You spend your birthday alone because your spouse can't get away from the office.	_____	_____	_____
15 You have to get a job to help with the expenses.	_____	_____	_____
16 A debt collector phoned the house three times in the past month.	_____	_____	_____
17 Your spouse was hanging around the house for two days last week because business was slow.	_____	_____	_____
18 Your spouse has been grouchy for a week because business has been bad.	_____	_____	_____
19 The telephone rings at all hours of the day and night with business calls.	_____	_____	_____
20 You have to help, and you know nothing about the business.	_____	_____	_____

Grade each Very displeased a 1, each Displeased a 2, and each Would understand a 3; then total the score.

If you believe your spouse would have scored between 51 and 60, you are fortunate in having an exceptionally supportive mate. Be very careful not to do anything that might erode the trust and confidence that is placed in you.

If you believe your spouse would score between 46 and 50, don't be disappointed because your marriage isn't perfect. Actually, this score rates between average and high average. It may indicate that you have a more realistic view of your marital relationship than the individual who came up with a higher total. Your spouse will likely be 'optimistically negative' about your new business venture. In your position, you can expect your spouse to be reasonably supportive, as long as you leave your work at the office, exercise normal judgement concerning your business prospects, and don't lose the family farm. Who could expect more than that?

If you scored your spouse's likely responses between 41 and 45, you're in the caution zone. Your score suggests a spouse likely to be 'pessimistically supportive' of the new business venture. Where another spouse might say, 'Go ahead if you think you're right,' yours would be likely to say. *'Don't* go ahead unless you're *sure* you're right.' Where another spouse might complain only when the business suffers minor failures, yours would be likely to complain about minor *successes* because they didn't measure up to expectations.

You will probably spend a lot of time defending your decision to go into business, in addition to the other business-related problems you can expect to encounter. Is this near-certain resistance on the home front worth it? Again, consider the question: which is most important — the business or the marriage?

Even if you believe your spouse will score 40 or less, go ahead and complete the quiz anyway. Use the quiz as a means of pinpointing areas that must be dealt with.

If you're absolutely determined to go into business, concentrate on finding ways you can eliminate some (hopefully most) of your spouse's reservations. If the big problem is money, try to find more capital before you make the jump. If it's time away from home, see if you can find a partner or the money to hire more help. As things stand, you're courting trouble if you simply ignore the warning signs and press forward on your own.

Through the looking glass

In case you're feeling self-satisfied and supremely confident at this point, hold on. You've performed a very rudimentary analysis of your spouse's *as you see it*. Now for the acid test.

Without any coaching on your part, give your spouse the test. Be fair. Don't stand and glare while the test is being taken. Don't impose a time limit. If your spouse isn't in the mood, wait until the time is right. Let it be known that you're looking for honest answers — any other kind will do neither of you any good in the long run.

After the test has been taken, see how your spouse's answers differ from those you expected them to be. Do you really know your spouse's feelings as well as you thought?

Discuss each area of difference at length and in detail. Remember, this is parlour game. It is a matter of critical importance to both of you!

Try your very hardest to reach a level of understanding that is comfortable and agreeable to each of you. Work at it!

Above all, realize that this is not the time for salesmanship. Your spouse cannot help feeling the way he or she feels, and you really are not going to be able to change those feelings very much, no matter how persuasive you may be. The purpose is not to convince, but to understand each other's views.

You may find that some of your differences stem from nothing more than a lack of knowledge. After all, this is *your* brainchild, not your spouse's. Provide your spouse with enough information about what you have in mind so that he or she can determine their feelings based on facts rather than emotions. Given all the facts, a hostile position might change into a supportive one. But again, remember that it's not to your advantage to 'sell' your opinion or to out-shout or deceive your spouse. You might win the round, but lose your ultimate objective — a successful business *and* a happy marriage. Talk to each other. Communicate. Share your hopes...and your fears.

Your still not home free.

Who else is deeply and personally involved with this decision? So much that your success — or failure — will have a profound impact on their lives? Your children? Your parents? A partner?

Why not see how each of those people will respond to this quiz? Be sure that they're absolutely honest with you when they take it. (Many people tend to tell you what they think you want to hear.) Discuss their concerns openly and at length. See if some of their reservations can't be overcome by making a minor revision in your game plan — for instance, by starting the business next year instead of this year. You may find that some of their concerns are well founded and that making modifications in your business plan actually will increase your chances of success.

Will you have a partner? How does the partner's spouse score on this quiz? If the partner's spouse isn't happy, you might lose the partner; and if you lose the partner, you might lose the business. Check it out before you take the plunge!

Family business

Value added tax (VAT) records show over 200,000 new registrations each year. There are over 1.4 million firms registered for VAT, 90 per cent of which have less than 200 employees and 70 per cent of these have less than 10 employees. These firms account for 40 per cent of the turnover of all firms and provide nearly half the total employment. Many of these firms are family owned and run. There are also about 2.6 million self-employed people in the UK, a figure which grew by 442,000 between 1981 and 1984.

Spouses tend to be valuable resources in operating a business. Spouses often invest in, own stock in, consult for, work in, and are officers and directors of family businesses. One study of medium-size firms indicated that up to 40 per cent of the companies include the spouse as an officer of the firm, while a slightly larger percentage include a spouse on the Board of Directors.

Do oil and water mix? In the study just mentioned, 64 per cent of the respondents said that having their spouses in the business had proved beneficial to their marriage.

2
Choosing a business

WHAT CAN YOU DO?

So far, we have explored some of the questions regarding your personal skills and attitudes, the commitment of your family and friends, and the strength of your own dedication to enter a business of your own. The next question is, What kind of business is right for you?

Two things take precedence over all others: are you considering a business that you *like?* And are you considering a business that you *know?*

People who are engaged in a business that they *like* tend to be happier, work harder, and be more successful. Going to work is fun for them, not a chore. Every accomplishment seems to have greater meaning. Minor setbacks don't seem to be as defeating as they might. At the very least, there's less of a tendency to sit around complaining or to wish that you were doing something (anything!) else.

But *liking* a business is no guarantee of success. You might *like* to make home movies, but that is hardly an indication that you could become a successful Hollywood producer. Select a business that you *know something about* — the more you know, the better. Trying to learn a business as you go can be as difficult and as frustrating as trying to play golf with one hand tied behind your back. Your competition is not going to make allowances for your lack of experience, and neither will your clientele. Don't make the mistake of gambling your career, your reputation, and your fortune on a longshot.

Beware of going into an overcrowded market with high costs and low revenues. The following industries seem to be nearing that point.

- Computerized bookkeeping services
- Biotechnology diagnostic kits
- Software retailing
- Mail order retailers
- Videocassettes hire and retail
- Vegetarian restaurants

Would anyone seriously consider going into a business that they don't know and like? As surprising as it may seem, people do it all the time. They may be swayed by a friend who remarks, 'You ought to get into computers; it's a wide-open field right now.' They may see a magazine advertisement that reads, 'Be your own boss, work at home, and earn £60,000 a year.' Or they may jump at the chance to buy the local printing services franchise, because 'there isn't a print shop in town.' And so, without knowing a thing about computers, printing or franchises, or whatever it is that supposedly will enable them to earn £60,000 a year working at home, these people make what may prove to be the biggest — and costliest — step of their lives. Don't be one of them!

Match or mismatch?

On occasion, an individual will have a strong desire for the benefits — real or perceived — or owning and operating a business, while the exact nature of that business may be rather obscure. For the moment, let's assume you are such a person.

How can you determine what kind of business would be right for you — a *match* rather than a *mismatch*?

Perhaps the most scientific approach would be to undergo some testing. Numerous examinations are available to help you determine whether your interests and abilities are in the arts or in mechanics, in jobs involving the use of your mind or in jobs involving the use of your hands. These tests do not take long to complete, and they are not expensive. Only you will have to know what the results are.

A do-it-yourself approach

The testing described above is revealing because it is specifically designed to look into things that a layman might tend to overlook or ignore. But you can make a thumbnail analysis of your interests and skills on your own, if you wish.

Begin by listing all the things that you liked best in school. These needn't necessarily be the subjects in which you got the best marks, although they will typically *not* be subjects in which you did poorly. Individuals' interests change as they grow older, and a particular interest — latent when you were in school — may blossom in later years. Don't forget to consider your extracurricular activities in school. This is List 1.

Next, make a list of all the things you have been trained to do — and like to do — since you left school — List 2.

Third, make a list of your hobbies and leisure activities — List 3.

Now, give a priority to each of the items on List 1. Put the thing you liked best at the top, followed by the thing you liked second best, and so on through the list.

Do the same thing with Lists 2 and 3.

Now the place the lists side by side and see what comparisons can be made. Look particularly for the similarities. Are there items that rank high on all three lists? Is there a way you can fit them into your thinking about a new business venture? Consider the possibilities in depth and length.

Put the lists in a desk drawer and refer to them from time to time. Ideas sometimes germinate slowly. An idea may pop into your mind on the fifth, the tenth, or the hundredth time you study the lists. If they don't actually supply the spark that gives you an idea for a business, they *can* be used when a business prospect comes to mind from another source. Do the skills and interests required for that business show up on your lists? If not, perhaps you're really not equipped to enter that field. Think about it.

A business that enables you to satisfy your personal needs rather than to sacrifice them stands the greatest likelihood of success. You're also apt to encounter less likelihood of burn-out further down the road.

FIRST, FIND A NEED

The essence of a successful business is its ability to fill a need in the market-place. If you are considering a business venture, you must first determine that there is a need for the product or service that you have in mind. This does not necessarily mean that you have to spend a lot of time and money on market research (depending on the complexity of your business, of course). Common sense can reveal a great deal.

By way of example, let's look at two different situations.

In Situation 1, you are considering opening a new retail grocery. Everyone needs to eat; therefore, the question of need seems obvious. But not necessarily! By looking into the situation more thoroughly, you discover that there are already more grocers in the area you have in mind than the market will sustain; in fact, two shops have closed down in the past year. To make matters worse, the population in your proposed market area has been declining steadily in recent years, meaning that there are fewer and fewer customers to be served. The need for food is unquestionable. The need for a new grocers is pretty unlikely.

In Situation 2, you are thinking about opening up a new bicycle shop. What is the outlook? Bicycles certainly are not a necessity; no one needs a bicycle to survive. On the other hand, you want to open your shop in an area with a large and growing concentration of families with children in the five- to thirteen-year-old bracket — and there's not another bicycle shop within thirty miles. The need for bicycles is so-so. But the need for a shop to serve this growing and untapped market is rather good.

Do not let enthusiasm interfere with your objective. Many people have failed in business simply be allowing their personal tastes to cloud their business judgement. You may be an ardent fan of vegetarian food, for example, and a gourmet chef, but if the local market wants sweet and sour pork or steak, a new vegetarian restaurant may not do very well. Suggestion: serve sweet and sour pork, or find another location for your vegetarian restaurant.

Remember that once you go into business you become the vendor. If you want to succeed, you will have to offer what the buyers want. Your taste may not agree with theirs, but the buyers call the shots. If you don't give them what they want, they'll simply go somewhere else.

It always helps to be flexible. If customers want beef Wellington instead of ratatouille give them beef Wellington.

It always helps to be flexible. If there's too much competition in the area, look for another area where there is little or no competition. Bend to the realities of the marketplace; don't expect the market-place to bend to suit you.

Time to review your situation

If you're still reading, you're presumably actively considering going into business. Many of the details may need to be worked out, and a definite timetable may not have been established, but you're certainly giving the possibility a great deal of thought.

This may be an excellent time to review your situation. Have you carefully considered what it would mean to give up your present job? Are you satisfied that you truly do have the self-discipline, the dedication, and the motivation to handle a business of your own? Have you identified a business that suits your talents and experience, and a business for which there is a genuine need in the marketplace? Do you have the support of your family, friends, and potential business associates?

Did you answer no to any of those questions? If so, stop now. Back up and begin again. You're not yet ready to go on.

If you answered yes to all those questions, you're probably ready to start on the hard part — taking the first real step toward turning your dream into a reality.

3
Should you start a business or buy one?

We must assume that finances are a major concern to anyone who is considering a new business. The objective is to satisfy your business needs while spending as little money as possible to do so. Sometimes it may be more economical to buy an existing business than to start a new one from scratch.

The advantages of starting a business from scratch may include:

- The ability to build or rent premises that are precisely the way you want them.
- The ability to equip and decorate your premises to suit your own needs and tastes.
- The ability to select a location of your own choice.
- The ability to staff the business as you choose.
- The ability to select a site that minimizes competition or one that will attract clientele from a nearby facility.
- The ability to start off with a clean slate.
- Additional ego gratification.
- The ability to add on to the business gradually, rather than to take on everything at once.
- Certain tax concessions or other financial inducements that may be available from the government.

The disadvantages of starting from scratch may include:

- It probably will take longer to get up to speed.
- The lack of an established customer base on which to build.
- The inability to find a suitable site.

- The inability to find suitable premises.
- The inability to find and recruit qualified personnel.
- Having to do everything from scratch, from naming the business to arranging for the phone to be connected.
- Having to make yourself known.
- The greater difficulty of establishing the necessary cash flow.

The advantages in buying an existing business may include:

- Acquiring certain legal rights, such as patents or copyrights.
- Acquiring an already-established customer base.
- Acquiring a good facility, on a good site, fully equipped and staffed for business.
- Acquiring a good business's reputation.
- Acquiring machinery and other valuable assets.
- Acquiring established and dependable sources of supply.
- Acquiring an established distribution system.
- Eliminating at least one competitor.

The disadvantages of buying an existing business may include:

- Acquiring premises and/or equipment which are old, run-down, or obsolete.
- Having to overcome the image of the previous management.
- Inheriting inept, poorly trained, overpaid, or unmotivated personnel.
- Inheriting an unfavourable union contract.
- Inheriting obsolete products.
- Inheriting the obligation — and cost — of servicing and maintaining products already in the field.
- Acquiring an excess of inventory.
- Having to take on the previous management's debt.
- Inheriting obsolete business systems, customer and financial records, and the like.
- Inheriting a number of unprofitable business contracts.
- Inheriting a weak board of directors.

The lists can go on and on. But these are all factors you must consider when making your decision.

Some factors may be so important as to outweigh all the

others. If your proposed business requires the use of a certain patented process, for example, and you're not allowed to license it, you may have to buy the company to get the patent. If you are planning to open a restaurant, on the other hand, and you intend to open it near a new shopping mall, there may be no other choice than to build one from scratch.

Some other considerations:

● Select a business for its future potential, not its past performance. Is it in the forefront of a new technology or at the tail end of an old one? Are sales, income, and profits rising or falling? Can you think of *specific ways* in which you can make the company grow?

● Buy the assets, if possible, and set your own values for depreciation. Are there customer complaints you should be aware of? Has the inventory been accurately and carefully valued? Are the building and equipment in good shape? Are all the key people planning to stay on? Get the sellers to sign a non-competition agreement to keep them from reopening under another name.

● Use intelligent financing. If possible get the seller to finance the buildings and equipment, perhaps under a leasing arrangement. Use a bank to finance the debtors and stock. See how much the company owes its employees in holiday entitlement or other wage and pension agreements. Know how much liability you are acquiring for employee severance pay and retirement agreements.

Buying a service business can be particularly tricky because the physical assets of the business may be less valuable than its goodwill — and how does one put a price on goodwill? A simple method is to value the firm's goodwill at the amount of its net profit over a specified period, usually two or three years.

Example: Mabel Miller was thinking of buying a company that provided contract cleaning services. The physical assets of the firm were worth £20,000, but the company had been in existence for a number of years, it had an excellent reputation, and it could offer Miller an established, loyal customer base. Since the firm had produced a net profit of £35,000 the previous year and £30,000 the year before that, the goodwill was valued at £65,000. Miller agreed to buy the company for £85,000.

Essentially, it's a game of checks and balances. You have certain objectives and you have a certain amount of money to invest. How can you gain the most and spend the least?

A thorough investigation of all your options is absolutely critical. This is particularly true if you are considering purchasing an existing business. You most certainly do not want to buy a business only to discover a month or two down the line that there's a major lawsuit hanging over it, or that the building you so badly wanted is to be torn down, or that the patent you desperately need is about to expire. The services of a good lawyer are essential.

THE LEVERAGED BUYOUT

Increasingly popular, it seems, is the leveraged buyout — a device whereby a company can be purchased largely on the basis of its own future earnings.

Prime candidates for a leveraged buyout are:

- Public companies that are trading at prices far below the value of their true net assets.
- Privately held companies with ageing management and no succession.
- Divisions or subsidiaries of corporations that do not, for one reason or another, fit into the parent company's future plans.

Candidates for a leveraged buyout are usually companies or businesses with a substantial base of hard assets (plant, equipment, accounts receivable, finished goods inventories). They have very little outstanding debt and a significant capacity for future borrowing. Their products are usually rather stable — not subject to immediate obsolescence or in need of major expenditures for research or product enhancements. They have a stable, though often not spectacular, history of growth and earnings. They have a good management team that will remain in place after the buyout.

Candidates for this type of acquisition usually are businesses producing net profits of about £500,000 after taxes with a sale price of eight to ten times their earnings.

There are professional investors who use the leveraged buyout as a means of acquisition and growth. But in many cases, the buyers are those who already are executives in — and are presently managing — the company. Combinations of an executive group and a professional investor are not uncommon.

Who benefits? The seller, who gets cash from the sale; the buyers, who gain equity in the company on borrowed capital; and the lender, who charges rates above the base rate on a loan that is exceptionally well secured by assets.

Since the debt-equity ratio of a company purchased in this manner is uncommonly high (10 : 1 not being unusual), there is considerable risk involved, particularly if much of the debt is short-term or carries an interest rate that is allowed to float with the base rate. Any business reversal, credit squeeze, or significant jump in the base rate could put the company in serious jeopardy.

Commonly, the new owners will take a company public within a few years. This adds considerably to the value of their equity in the firm. But in order to have a successful initial public offering, the firm must be able to reduce its debt-to-equity ratio substantially and maintain the company's earnings at or above the projected levels.

WHAT ABOUT A FRANCHISE?

Except in the field of manufacturing, there are franchises for practically everything these days — accounting services, equipment rental, every type of fast food. In a sense, even an independently owned petrol station is a franchise.

The USA is well ahead of Britain in franchises; in 1982, franchises accounted for 34 per cent of all retail sales, according to the Department of Commerce, by taking in a total of $383.9 billion. Car and lorry dealers accounted for roughly half of these, and petrol stations accounted for approximately one-third, but franchised convenience stores, restaurants, and other retailers were responsible for some $67.7 billion in sales for the year. In Britain, franchising is a fast-growing area. There are over 300 franchises on sale, requiring initial capital of a few thousand to a quarter of a million pounds.

Franchises offer many advantages.

- They have a built-in reputation for you to trade on.
- If you don't know anything about the business, they will teach you and even help you train your staff.
- They will help you select a good site.
- They will design, equip, and (in some cases) help you build your facility.
- They will help you promote your business.
- They will give you a step-by-step guide on how to run a profitable operation.
- If you later decide to sell out, they will even help you find a buyer, or they will buy your business from you themselves.

But bear in mind: you pay for what you get!

Opening a franchise hamburger outlet today may cost you well over £250,000. Once you're up and running, you will continue to pay a percentage of your profits (or your gross) to the franchising corporation. You also may be required to contribute a percentage to the local or regional franchisees' organization.

You will also sacrifice a considerable amount of your business freedom. The franchise company may send inspectors to check on you. You will have to submit detailed financial reports. You will be expected to include new products or services as they are introduced, to participate in special promotions, and to follow the company's guidelines to a T. Failure to do so may cause you to lose your franchise.

Still, franchises are a reasonably safe and sure method of going into business, especially if you lack business experience, special talents or skills, or a marketable product or service of your own on which to base a business.

Be advised that many franchising systems have not made the grade, however. For every McDonald's, Pizza Hut, or Snap-On Tools, there is an Arthur Treacher's or some other seemingly good idea that went sour.

Investigate the situation before you invest. Ensure that the franchise contract sets out the commitments of both parties in full, and look for clear support from the franchiser during the early stages of the business. The more established franchises are members of the British Franchise Association whose address is in Appendix 1. The safest investments are those that have a long, well-established track record — but they're also the most expensive. Newer franchising operations, especially in an unproven field, may be less expensive to invest in, but they will also involve a greater degree of risk.

The franchising organization may be risking its reputation on you, but you are risking your money on them. Be careful!

THE COTTAGE INDUSTRIES

More and more people are working out of their homes.

The so-called cottage industries are gaining wide appeal from those who:

- are tired of commuting;
- are disenchanted with larger companies;
- want more time with their families;
- want a more active role in raising their children;
- want a greater degree of self-determination;
- enjoy the freedom and challenge of being their own boss;
- have found a more satisfying means of self-expression.

Among the benefits are:

- fewer interruptions;
- less expense for clothing, transportation, and restaurant lunches;
- a more flexible work schedule.

Among the drawbacks are:

- the need for extreme self-discipline;
- a feeling of isolation from the outside world;
- a strong reliance on personal funding to run the business;
- problems with planning permission, or tenants' agreements in using a home as business premises.

Although legalities may pose problems in some areas, particularly if your activity offends the neighbours, local councils are usually supportive. There are many activities which can be carried out at home such as writing, bookkeeping, jewellery making, upholstery, assembly work, teaching, computer programming. The list is endless. If you are acting as an outworker or homeworker for one firm only, the Inland Revenue may class you as an employee and not as self-employed. This will affect your tax position.

Linda Jones
LDJ Design and Display

For some people, Christmas lasts all year round! Take Linda Jones, for example. In 1980 Linda was a pen-pushing clerk in the DHSS, then she got a job display-merchandising Christmas decorations in department stores. This led on to greater things, as designer of the local authority's Christmas illuminations programme where she saw a tremendous growth potential for the use of outdoor Christmas decorations in the ubiquitous town shopping centres.

Although she had no formal training in design, she had flair, was not afraid of hard work, and was willing to give it a go. So, with very little cash, she launched her business in 1985 at the age of 27. At first, she offered consultancy services to local authorities and shopping centres helping them design, source and put up the decorations. By year two however, demand was so great she was having her decorations made by sub-contractors and was offering a full design-build-install service.

In year two, Linda's brother David joined her in partnership and with their combined expertise they went from strength to strength. LDJ's decorations brightened the shopping precincts of major cities up and down the country. Although local government spending was being cut overall, they were still spending to attract tourists and customers for local traders. Linda was on to a winner.

This Christmas Linda's decorations will be in six cities, and over 40 shopping precincts. Her company, LDJ Design and Display Ltd., now employs five people full time with various sub-contractors and outworkers. A move to larger premises is now necessary to cope with the increased sales and services that are being offered under the LDJ banner and, 'Next year', says Linda, 'we are going to top the half-million sales.' Running your own business is great fun, but as Linda adds, 'It helps if you are a little "crackers".'

4
Preparing your business plan

Although many businesses fail because of bad management or inadequate financing, the major cause of business failure overall is probably a lack of proper planning. What is management, after all, but planning? And adequate planning should certainly reveal — and enable management to deal with — the financial well-being of the company.

Planning is an on-going process, and it never ends. You develop a plan for getting a business started, then you develop a plan to cover its operation and growth. A well-run company will modify its plans project by project, year by year, sometimes month by month.

Plans are not static. They need to be flexible. They need to change as your company changes, as the market changes, as competition changes. Plans should be designed to help you move, not to prohibit your movement. Never allow your business plan to become a strait-jacket.

Plans are not autocratic commandments from on high, to be executed blindly by the company's personnel. Rather, they should be democratic instruments, prepared with the input and counsel of your employees.

A good business plan will provide a systematic guideline for running the business. It will provide you with the information you need to make key decisions and will give your personnel a clear understanding of your goals. It will furnish your employees with a clear understanding of their responsibilities for meeting the company goals.

It will provide the employees with a way to help the business to succeed by offering them a way to participate in the development, as well as the implementation, of the plan, and it will give your employees, your suppliers, your customers, your investors, and youself more confidence that you know what you're doing and that you know where you're going. Finally, it will be a valuable tool in hiring top-level personnel.

Most of these things will evolve later, Part II (refer to page 63) goes into business planning in greater detail. Right now, we're concerned principally with the development of a plan that will help you to get your new business off the ground.

MAKING A BUSINESS PLAN

Using the outline below for a guide, elaborate on your business plan as fully as possible. Don't look for short, pat answers; rather use as much detail, as many facts and figures, and as many specifics as you can.

Allow yourself plenty of time to do a thorough job. The thoroughness you demonstrate here will pay off in the weeks and months ahead.

Business plan outline

Summary
1 Description of the business
 (a) Name
 (b) Location(s) of factory/shop/office
 (c) Product or service
 (d) Personnel
 (e) Market
 (f) Competition
 (g) Management experience/skills
2 Business goals
3 Financial needs and utilization of funds
4 Earnings projections
5 Potential return to investors
Manufacturing process (if applicable)
1 Machinery and facilities
2 Materials

3 Sources of supply
4 Production methods

Products or services
1 Description of product line(s)
2 Comparison to competitors' products or services
3 Proprietary position
   (a) Patents
   (b) Copyrights
   (c) Other legal or technical considerations

Market analysis
1 Description of total market
2 Competiton
3 Industry trends
4 Target market

Marketing strategy
1 Overall strategy
2 Your product or service
   (a) Method of selling
   (b) Method of distributing
   (c) Method of servicing
3 Pricing policy

Management plan
1 Form of business structure
2 Composition of Board of Directors (if any)
3 Officers
   (a) Organization chart
   (b) Names
   (c) Titles and responsibilities
   (d) Individual backgrounds
4 Staffing plan
   (a) Number of employees
   (b) Deployment of personnel
5 Facilities plan
   (a) Description of existing or initial facility
   (b) Plans for capital improvements
6 Operating plan
   (a) Orders in hand at start-up
   (b) Prospective business on hand at start-up
   (c) Schedule of work projected over next two years

Financial data
1 Financial statement for past five years (if you are purchas-

ing an existing business)

2 First-year financial projection by quarters
   (a) Profit and loss statements (refer to Chapter 11)
   (b) Balance sheets (see example page 39)
   (c) Cash-flow charts (see sample page 40)
   (d) Estimates of capital expenditures

3 Annual financial projections for years two to five
   (a) Profit and loss statements (see p. 140)
   (b) Balance sheets (see p. 39)
   (c) Cash-flow charts (see p. 40)
   (d) Estimates of capital expenditures

4 Explanation of projections

5 Key business ratios

6 Explanations of use and effect of funds

7 Return to investors
   (a) Projected for company
   (b) Comparison to industry as a whole

Don't hesitate to get help in preparing your business plan. You want the best input you can get. Your potential partners, employees, or investors should be able to help. So should potential members of your Board of Directors, if you propose to have one. Banks and accounting firms have people who can help, as do professional associations and similar industry groups or societies. Your local Enterprise Agency or Small Firms Service counsellor can also help you prepare the plan. There is also a variety of training offered by colleges and consultants which will bring you up to date with the jargon used in business plans. Some business schools run programmes to support you through the process of building up the plan. Most of this training is subsidized by the government. See Appendix 4 for further details.

The very process of preparing this plan will raise — and hopefully help you to answer — many critical business questions. The more problems you solve before you get into business, the fewer problems you will have later. If you uncover a question that you can't answer, hold up until you can. Initiating a business venture when you have holes in your business plan is as foolish as setting out on a motor trip with two flat tyres. Remember the old adage: if you don't know where you're going, any road will take you there.

If you are going to need financing, this business plan is absolutely essential. The more thorough it is, the more likely you will be able to get the money you need from a responsible lending institution.

A QUICK REVIEW

Preparing a business plan can be very difficult, particularly if you have never done one before. Perhaps these additional questions will be helpful:

Product(s) or service(s)

- Have you fully described the basic science or technology that goes into the manufacture of your product (or performance of your service)?
- Is there anything new or unique about it?
- Can you foresee any technological developments over the next few years that might favourably or unfavourably affect it?
- What need does your product or service fulfil?
- How is that need currently being satisfied?
- How is your product or service different from those presently available?
- Is there some other way in which this need can be served, and if so, what are its advantages and disadvantages?
- What is the life expectancy of your product or service in the market-place?
- Are you unfavourably dependent on one source of supply for materials or labour? (To find other suppliers, consult a buyers' guide or directory at your local library.) Examples are *Kelly's Directory*, *Stubbs Buyer's Guide* and, of course, the *Yellow Pages*.
- Are you planning any new products or services that should be delineated and included in your business plan?

Market analysis

- Have you used every available source in attempting to forecast the size of the market for your product or service over the next ten-year span?

- Have you been realistic in forecasting what share of the market you can expect during each of those years?
- If you propose to serve more than one market, have you identified and analysed each and all of them?
- Who are your current competitors, and what market share currently is held by each? What factors may cause one or more of them to gain — or lose — some of their share?
- What are your competitors' strengths and weaknesses?
- Are there likely to be more competitors in the near future? Why? How can that affect your business?
- What is the biggest single stumbling block to your entry into the market? How do you plan to overcome it? How are your competitors likely to react?

Marketing strategy

- Are any of your sales secured by contract? What are the particulars? Are you protected if you suffer a major catastrophe, such as an act of God?
- How did you arrive at your sales forecast?
- How did you determine the price of your product or service?
- What are your costs? How did you determine them?
- Do you have a specific plan for growing the business? (Avoid saying: 'Well, the industry is growing by 15 per cent a year, so we will grow 15 per cent a year.')
- How do you propose to evaluate your progress?
- Are you prepared to modify your business plan, if necessary?
- Do you have a contingency plan ready in case your first plan doesn't work?
- Have you thoroughly checked out your position relative to patents, copyrights, licensing agreements, trade secrets, and similar legalities, not only for your product or service, but for the company as a whole, and for the manner in which you intend to do business? Are these things described in your business plan?
- Have you described the organization of your marketing staff? How many people will be required? What skills

and experience do they need? Do you have or can you hire the quality and number of people you need?

- Do you plan to change your marketing strategy or structure along the way? Why? How? When?
- Who will determine your marketing strategy?
- Who will make your marketing decisions?
- Will your marketing personnel also provide customer or product service? How are they to be trained?
- If your marketing people don't do it, who will provide customer and/or product service?
- Have you provided for guarantees or warranties on your product or service?

Management plan

- Have you fully explored the advantages and disadvantages of each 'structural' option (becoming a limited company rather than forming a partnership, for example)? Have you committed your conclusions to paper and included them in your business plan?
- Are you flexible enough to accept an alternate business structure if you discover that your first choice is impractical?
- Do you foresee changing the company's business structure in the future? Why? When? How?

Buying a business

- How long has the firm been in business?
- How good is the company's reputation?
- How efficiently has the company been run?
- Why does the company exist? What is special about it?
- Do you plan to change the business in any way? Why? When? How? What effect will the change(s) have on the market, your customer base, your competition?
- What are the specific weaknesses of the company? How do you propose to overcome them?
- What are the physical requirements of the company as you propose to run it (plant size, equipment, land area, transportation, utilities, and so on)? How do these match up with what there is now? How do you propose

to finance any changes or improvements?

- Is the location suitable to your needs (access to labour, suppliers, transportation, customers)?
- How big does the company wish to become? (Be realistic. Even if you're in a multi-million pound industry, you can't expect to capture it all!)
- What fringe benefits will you offer your personnel? Have you budgeted for them?
- How can you be sure your suppliers are reliable? Do you have secondary sources for anything that is critical?
- Have you fully described your distribution plans?
- Have you considered how pricing, taxes, environment, and other regulatory considerations will affect the company? Their advantages? Disadvantages?
- Have you considered the ways in which any changes in those regulations (pricing, taxes, environment, and so on) might affect the company? Advantages? Disadvantages?
- What geographic penetration do you envision (local, regional, national, international)? Will that change in time? When? How?

Financial plan

- Even if you have the start-up capital, do you have (or have access to) enough additional capital to cover operating expenses? How long can you afford to operate at a loss? How long can you operate at the break-even point?
- When can you reasonably expect to turn a profit?
- How much profit, both in pounds and as a percentage of sales, do you feel you need to be successful?
- If you acquired an existing business but intend to make significant changes in it (converting a Chinese restaurant into a vegetarian restaurant, for example), how will the change affect your forecasts? Have you based the forecasts on the business as it is or on the business as you expect it to be? Have you anticipated the loss of some customers (income) while you're in the process of attracting new ones?
- If you plan to introduce a new product or service, have you taken into account a budget to cover research and

development, new tooling, employee training, advertising, and so on?
- Have you planned properly for equipment maintenance, depreciation, and replacement?
- Have you included a factor for waste or spoilage in your plans?
- Have you budgeted for new product development? For promotion? For employee training?
- Do you have firm cost quotes from your suppliers? Are they guaranteed by contract?
- Have you provided financially for warranty or product liability expenses?
- What is the total cost of your proposed venture? How much of it will have to be financed? Have you budgeted for the cost of this financing?
- What portion of these funds do you expect to raise from debt rather than equity?
- If you will require financing, have you described in detail how this money is to be spent?
- Does your financial plan include a detailed description of your financial history (assets, liabilities, credit history)?
- What is your financial year to be?

Table 1
Andrea's Club Marin
Balance sheets

	Actual Sept 1988		Projected Sept 1989	
	£	£	£	£
Equity		20,000	—	20,000
Add net profit	—		20,735	
Less drawings	—		14,000	
Less tax	—	—	1,000	5,735
Total owner's equity	—	20,000		25,735
Loans		60,000	60,000	
Less repayments		—	5,108	54,829
		80,000		80,627

Balance sheet continued
Fixed Assets

Equipment	16,200		16,200	
Less depreciation	—	16,200	3,000	13,200
Goodwill		58,000		58,000
		74,200		71,200
Deposits		1,300		1,300
Current assets				
Stock	—		5,000	
Debtors	—		4,760	
Bank	4,500		13,157	
Total	4,500		22,917	
Less current liabilities				
Trade creditors	—		14,250	
Expense creditors	—		540	
Total	—		14,790	
Net current assets		4,500		8,127
		80,000		80,627

Table 2
Andrea's Club Marin
Projected profit and loss statement
Oct 1988 — Sept 1989

		£
Sales		208,000
Less cost of sales		157,230
Gross profit		50,770
Expenses		
Salaries	7,920	
Overheads	13,200	
Depreciation	3,000	
Interest	5,915	30,035
Net profit		20,735

Table 3
Andrea's Club Marin
Projected Fund Flow

	Pre-operating	1986 Oct.	Nov.	Dec
Cash sources				
Equity	20,000			
Loan	60,000			
Net profit	0	478	1,001	2,234
Depreciation	0	250	250	250
Total	80,000	728	1,251	2,484
Disbursements				
Purchase of business	58,000			
Closing Costs	1,200			
Improvements and Equipment	15,000			
Deposits	1,300			
Loan payments (Principal)	0	406	410	413
Owner's drawings	0	1,000	1,000	1,200
Income taxes	0			
Total	75,500	1,406	1,410	1,613
Net Fund Flow	4,500	(678)	(159)	871
Cumulative fund flow	4,500	3,822	3,663	4,534

1987

Jan.	Feb.	Mar.	Apr.	May	June	July	Aug.	Sept.	Total
									20,000
									60,000
1,738	1,491	1,745	1,749	1,752	2,006	2,010	2,264	2,267	20,735
250	250	250	250	250	250	250	250	250	3,000
1,988	1,741	1,995	1,999	2,002	2,256	2,260	2,514	2,517	103,735
									58,000
									1,200
									15,000
									1,300
416	420	424	427	431	434	439	442	446	5,108
1,200	1,200	1,200	1,200	1,200	1,200	1,200	1,200	1,200	14,000
			1,000						1,000
1,616	1,620	1,624	2,627	1,631	1,634	1,639	1,642	1,646	95,608
372	121	371	(628)	371	622	621	872	871	8,127
4,906	5,027	5,398	4,770	5,141	5,763	6,384	7,256	8,127	

Table 4
Andrea's Club Marin

	1988 Oct.	Nov.	1989 Dec.	Jan.	Feb.
Income					
Cash Sales	10,000	11,000	13,000	12,000	11,000
Debtors (note 1)	0	5,000	5,000	6,000	5,000
Total Income (A)	10,000	16,000	18,000	18,000	16,000
Outgoings					
Creditor payments (note 2)	0	17,000	12,480	14,250	12,750
Salaries	600	600	600	600	600
National Insurance (note 3)	0	60	60	60	60
Alarm Service	180				
Advertising	80	80	80	80	80
Delivery	20	20	20	20	20
Dues and Subscriptions	120				
Laundry and Linen	10	10	10	10	10
Legal and Accounting					
Office expenses	10	10	10	10	10
Repairs and Maintenance	200				200
Supplies	35	35	35	35	35
Phone			105		
Utilities			300		
Miscellaneous	50	50	50	50	50
Insurance	1,200				
Rent	300	300	300	300	300
Licences	1,500				
Loan Interest	512	509	506	502	499
Loan repayment	406	410	413	416	420
Income tax					
Owners drawings	1,000	1,000	1,200	1,200	1,200
Total outflow (B)	6,223	20,084	16,169	17,533	16,234
Net cashflow (A-B)	3,777	−4,084	1,831	467	−234
Starting cash	4,500				
Cumulative total	8,277	4,193	6,024	6,491	6,257

Projected Cash Flow Forecast
Prepared August 1st 1988
All figures in £s

Mar.	Apr.	May	June	July	Aug.	Sept.	Total
12,000	12,000	12,000	13,000	13,000	14,000	14,000	147,000
5,000	5,000	5,000	5,000	5,000	5,000	5,000	56,000
17,000	17,000	17,000	18,000	18,000	19,000	19,000	203,000
12,000	12,750	12,750	12,750	13,500	13,500	14,250	14,980
600	600	600	600	600	600	600	7,200
60	60	60	60	60	60	60	660
							180
80	80	80	80	80	80	80	960
20	20	20	20	20	20	20	240
							120
10	10	10	10	10	10	10	120
	600					600	1,200
10	10	10	10	10	10	10	120
			200				600
35	35	35	35	35	35	35	420
105			105			105	420
300			300			300	1,200
50	50	50	50	50	50	50	600
							1,200
300	300	300	300	300	300	300	3,600
							1,500
495	491	488	484	480	476	473	5,915
424	427	431	434	439	442	446	5,108
	1,000						1,000
1,200	1,200	1,200	1,200	1,200	1,200	1,200	14,000
15,689	17,633	16,034	16,638	16,784	16,783	18,539	194,343
1,311	−633	966	1,362	1,216	2,217	461	8,657
							4,500
7,568	6,935	7,901	9,263	10,479	12,696	13,157	13,157

Notes to Table 4

Note 1
About one-third of sales are made on credit. These bills are paid by customers during the following month.

Note 2
Creditors are paid in the month following the purchase of the goods. An initial stock worth £5,000 was purchased in October and paid for in November.

Note 3
Deductions for National Insurance made from the wages are sent to the Collector of Taxes in the following month. Value Added Tax has been ignored.

Note 4
Some expenses are not made regularly throughout the year, but are paid periodically.

Part II

Getting the business started

5
The structure of your business

You have the plan. You have the commitment. Now what do you have to do?

Typically, one of your first legal considerations will be to determine what type of business *structure* to have. You may already have been forced to consider this question while working on your business plan. In any event, you should be aware that a business may legally be structured in a number of ways, and that there are certain advantages and disadvantages to each of them. You will want to select the one that is most suitable for you.

Do not presume that you can handle this decision alone, and do not think that you can draw up your own papers by copying those of another, similar business; or by using standard, pre-printed forms sometimes found in office supplies; or by following the directions in one of those do-it-yourself books. One of these follies might save you some money at the start, but you're almost sure to pay the price later. The advice of a good accountant and a good commercial solicitor is essential. The law is constantly changing and they have the experience and legal obligation to do things the right way.

Essentially there are five basic business structures on which to base your business: the sole proprietorship, the partnership, the limited company (Ltd), the co-operative, and the public limited company (plc).

SOLE PROPRIETORSHIP

This is the simplest of all business structures. In a sense, it does not involve a real 'organization' because the owner (proprietor) *is* the business and vice versa. Legally, the two are one and the same. As the sole proprietor, you have full and direct control over all aspects of your business.

To establish a sole proprietorship, all that may be necessary is:

- Registering with the local tax inspector on Form 41G.
- Informing the local Department of Social Security office.

You may also want to check with the Planning Officer that your premises are suitable, and with the Customs and Excise to see if you should register for value added tax.

You need not register any business name but the owner's name as well as the business name must appear on all business stationery. Also on this stationery must be an address at which documents could be served, which, or course, is usually the business address.

Actually, one person may operate a number of companies simultaneously as sole proprietor, and each of those companies may use a different accounting system. The point is, the assets of the company(ies) are the assets of the *individual*, and they must be reported as such on the individual's personal income tax return.

You may not split the income from the business among various members of your family unless those members of the family actually work in the business and draw a salary.

The owner will be taxed on the profits of the business, including the salary taken from them, at the normal rates of income tax. National Insurance contribution payments are generally lower than those paid by employed people, but the benefits available are less. An owner can take advantage of most of the business deductions available to other forms of business, including normal expenses and pension schemes. The exact rules change frequently, so you should take professional advice from an accountant about your own circumstances.

Of course, as a sole proprietor you have unlimited liability for the obligations of the business. Its debts are your debts. Legal action resulting from injury to people or property caused by your products — or by your employees — are yours to deal with. Similarly, charges that your product or service does not perform or that it is not what it is represented to be are yours to resolve. As a sole proprietor, you are putting not only the assets of your business on the line but your personal assets as well.

Insurance is available to protect you from these risks, but it can be costly, depending on the type of business you are in. In many cases, it's also possible to protect your non-business assets by signing by them over to a spouse or some other party. Here again, the advice of a good commercial solicitor is invaluable.

If you choose to form a sole proprietorship, it is wise to separate the assets of the business from any other assets you may possess. Use a separate bank account for operating the business, and specify in your will how the assets of the business are to be handled in the event of your death.

One of the principal disadvantages to the sole proprietorship structure, in addition to the personal liability involved, is that the owner must report all of the business profits as direct income on his or her personal income tax. This may cause you to pay more taxes than you would pay if the business were incorporated. Of course, many new businesses operate at a loss for a period of time, in which case you can use those losses to offset any other income you may have, and subject to Inland Revenue restrictions, you may even be able to carry the losses back (to obtain a refund from previous income taxes) or carry them forward (to lessen the amount of taxes that you will have to pay in the future).

PARTNERSHIP

Partnerships are formed when two or more people join together to conduct business. All partners are jointly and severally liable for the obligations of the business. Individuals, corporations, and existing partnerships may participate in forming a partnership.

A partnership is as easy to form as a sole proprietorship. A written partnership agreement is not even required, although one is strongly recommended to set forth the rights and responsibilities of each partner. Such an agreement can be particularly valuable if and when the partnership is dissolved, or if there is a death among the partners.

A partnership is similar to a sole proprietorship, in that all the partners are jointly liable for the debts and obligations of the

business. Creditors can look to the assets of any one of the partners to fulfil all the obligations of the partnership, and any
agreement among the partners to share this responsibility,
although binding on them, is not binding on the creditors.

Partnerships have a limited life, the terms of which may be set
forth in the partnership agreement. Also, the death, incapacity,
bankruptcy, or withdrawal of any partner automatically ter-
minates the partnership unless otherwise specified in the partnership agreement.

In start-up situations, a partnership may offer some advantages. Operating losses may be deducted by the partners from
their individual income taxes. Certain items of income and certain deductions may be allocated to a specific partner, subject to
the requirements of the law, and this could provide a substantial
economic benefit. The partnership may borrow funds from a
third-party creditor.

Any partner may transfer his interest to someone else, unless
forbidden to do so by the partnership agreement. On the death
of a partner, her interest in the business will be transferred
according to the terms of a will.

The choice of a partner should not be taken lightly. Like a
good spouse, a good partner will be a true helpmate, encouraging you, taking many burdens off your shoulders, and providing
support during the good times and the bad. A poor partnership
can cause you as much grief as a bad marriage.

Look for these qualities in selecting a business partner:

- *A comfortable 'chemistry'.* Does the partner stimulate
  enthusiasm? Does the partner stimulate new ideas? Can
  you work well together? Is there an absence of ego,
  authoritarianism, and stubbornness?
- *Different backgrounds.* Can the partner offer a different
  perspective? Can you disagree agreeably? Can you both
  use logic, rather than emotion, to reconcile differences?
  Does the partner add a talent of some experience to the
  business that you do not have?
- *A willingness to share the same goals.* Can you pull
  together as a team? Do you have similar outlooks
  towards the company, where it should go, and how to
  get there? Are you about equal in drive and ambition?
  If you plan to form a proprietorship, there is little else
  to do. You're virtually 'on the road'.

If you plan to form a partnership, we strongly recommend the preparation of a partnership agreement, *although this is not required by law*. In it, you might consider including the following:

1 *An allocation of the management authority and responsibility*. Decide *who* is to be responsible for what. All of the partners do not have to have a hand in the management of the business. Above all, decide *who is to be the boss*.

2 *A definition of the financial details*. What cash or property is being transferred to the partnership? By which of the partners? What *value* is being placed on the property that is being transferred? Are any of the partners to contribute additional capital later? On what terms? What are the consequences if they fail to do so? Are partners to make loans to the firm? On what terms? What are the consequences if they fail to do so? What percentage of the income, gains, losses, and deductions from the business is to be allocated to each partner? (All need not be treated equally, of course.)

3 *A definition of transfers and terminations*. Can the partners transfer their interests to outsiders? If so, on what basis? If not, how are those interests to be handled by the remaining partner(s) in the event one partner wants to leave? (Reminder: unless your partnership agreement states otherwise, a partnership is dissolved when any one partner leaves or dies.) Is the partnership to terminate on the retirement, death, incompetency, insanity, or bankruptcy of any one partner? If not, how will that partner's interests be handled? How will that partner's responsibilities to the company be absorbed by the remaining partner(s)?

It should be pointed out that any business may begin as a sole proprietorship, a general partnership, or a limited partnership and incorporate at some later time.

It is also wise to remember that no business can have two bosses. One person must be in charge. Although income may be divided equally between two partners, as well as the workload, someone must be in control. If you are considering the partnership form of business, it may be necessary to set your ego aside and have the better business partner actually direct the company.

CO-OPERATIVES

A co-operative has as its philosophy, that workers should also be owners. In fact, only half the workers in a co-operative need be owners, but the minimum number of members, if it is to be formed under the Industrial and Provident Societies Acts 1965-75, is seven.

The management, objectives and use of the assets must be controlled by its workforce. A voting system must be defined (e.g., one vote per member). The profits must be shared among the workforce, after any interest is paid to those providing finance. It is therefore difficult to attract long-term investors. Generally speaking, this form of business will not give you an opportunity for great wealth creation, but is found to be highly satisfactory to groups of motivated people.

Co-operative groups can of course form partnerships or limited companies. Further information can be obtained from the Co-operative Development Agency. (See appendix 1 for details). There are also many local CDA's now. You can find these in your *Yellow Pages*.

INCORPORATION

Limited companies are formed according to the stringent requirements of company law. This makes it absolutely essential for you to engage sound legal advice if you choose to incorporate.

A limited liability company is an entity (a person) in its own right. It must pay taxes, it must abide by a strict set of laws and regulations, it may incur debt, and it may go into liquidation.

Incorporating as a limited company is a common and versatile way of conducting a business. It is a legal entity, separate and apart from its owners. For example, the owners may change but the business remains legally the same business. A limited company is managed through a board of directors, who are elected by the shareholders, and the board then selects the officers who will actually operate the business. The directors may or may not be shareholders. Generally speaking, they will be responsible for making major business and policy decisions, while the officers make decisions on the company's day-to-day operations. The officers may or may not be shareholders. A limited company must have at least two shareholders, of whom at least one must be a director. It must also have a company secretary who could be the other director, another shareholder or a professional, such as an accountant.

A limited company must keep its own business records, prepare its own tax returns, and pay its own taxes. It is also responsible for its own debts — the shareholders are *not* liable for the obligations of the company.

It is more difficult to incorporate a business than to set up a proprietorship or partnership. It is a job for a solicitor. The company has to be registered with the Registrar of Companies. Once registered, the company is given a Certificate of Incorporation which has to be displayed publicly. The registration number must appear on the company's stationery.

The main documents which are registered are the *Memorandum* and the *Articles of Association*. The name of the company must be approved by the Registrar, and this will be shown in the Memorandum, as will the location of the head office and details of the share capital, including the extent of the liabilities. The Memorandum also includes the Objects — what the company is for and what it can do. These should be wide enough to allow for developments, but not so wide that it ends up doing things which the shareholders would not wish it to. The Articles of Association (normally called the Articles) set out the rules for the internal management of the firm, for example, what voting rights particular directors have. It can take several weeks and several hundreds of pounds to set up a new company. A quicker and cheaper way is to buy one 'off the shelf'. The name can then be changed in about three weeks.

THE BOARD OF DIRECTORS

Only limited companies and public limited companies are required to have a board of directors, but proprietorships and partnerships may find it extremely helpful to form some similar group (committee, panel, forum) to provide them with valuable business advice.

The corporate board of directors has the responsibility of managing — or directing the management of — the company. They are elected (usually each year) by the shareholders. They, in turn, elect the officers of the company.

As an entrepreneur, the composition of the board should be of extreme importance to you.

When a company is first formed, the founding shareholders often elect themselves to the board of directors. But, as the company grows, it often becomes useful to have access to outside experience or expertise. People who have demonstrated strength in certain critical areas of business are frequently added to the board. If you are going to require capital, for example, perhaps a banker should be on the board. If you are going to be involved in a great many legalities, perhaps a solicitor would be valuable on the board. If you are weak in marketing, perhaps a marketing expert should be on your board.

Although it is not in the nature of the 'go it alone' entrepreneur to involve these non-executive directors, they can maintain more objectivity when considering important decisions. Many institutional investors insist on placing a non-executive director on the board.

The board of directors is the shareholders' panel of experts, their 'brains trust'. The more competent its members, the greater the chances of success of the business.

In time, some companies grow to great size and complexity. They acquire staffs of financial experts, lawyers, and marketing personnel. Their operations branch off into a number of divisions, or they acquire certain subsidiaries. When that occurs, the shareholders sometimes prefer to elect an *internal* board of directors, which might include the company secretary (in lieu of an outside banker), the head of the legal department (in lieu of an outside solicitor), or the head of the marketing department (in lieu of an outside marketing expert). Or the internal board might be composed of the heads of each major operating division or subsidiary.

The idea is that the inside people may combine the expertise of the outside expert with the greater familiarity that they have with the company itself. The shareholders must weigh that possibility the possibility that insiders may be too close to the forest to see the trees and that outsiders may be able to introduce some fresh thinking or a different point of view to the board. Many corporations have both insiders and outsiders on the board.

One's ability to control the makeup of the board may change as time goes by. In order to help a business grow, the founding shareholders may relinquish more and more of their equity in the company to other investors (after all, 10,000 shares valued at twenty pounds each are worth more than 100,000 shares valued at one pound each), but in a situation in which there are 100,000 shares of voting stock in the company, ownership of 100,000 shares provides absolute control over the selection of the board, whereas ownership of 10,000 shares provides the owner(s) with only one-tenth of the company's voting power. Those who control the other 90 per cent of the voting stock can easily outvote the company's original founders.

The powers of the board

When a company is incorporated, the board of directors, not the officers, becomes the governing body of the organization. The board makes or delegates the authority to make such decisions as purchasing new property or equipment, entering into various legal contracts, or issuing new stock. It hires and fires the company's officers. Through the authority vested in the directors by the company's owners (shareholders), they *are* the corporation.

But if their power is great, so are the directors' responsibilities. They are the trustees of the company, charged to protect the shareholders' interests and act in the best interests of the company they serve. Any errors of omission or commission in office can make them — singly or collectively — subject to legal action by the shareholders.

Directors must be continuously aware of the activities of the company. They must be able to make informed decisions about the corporation, and they must be alert to outside factors that may be either beneficial or detrimental to the corporation. They are expected to attend the meetings of the board.

A director may not take advantage of his or her position by taking business that otherwise might have gone to the corporation, by entering into an unfair contract or participating in an unfair transaction with the corporation, or by using insider information to buy or sell the company's shares in a manner that is advantageous to himself or herself but detrimental to the company.

A director may not allow the company to make an unlawful payment of dividends (paying a dividend when there is not adequate funds for that purpose) or to make an unlawful distribution of its assets (distributing them to the shareholders without making provision for paying the company's debts).

Directors should read and become thoroughly acquainted with the Articles of Association and Memorandum of their company — these effectively set out the rules for the business; what it can and cannot do. They should also be aware of their duties under the various Companies Acts.

Some close advisers to the company may also be under the same legal obligations as directors to ensure the proper behaviour of the company. These so-called 'shadow directors' are not appointed as such, but their behaviour might be *interpreted* as such by the law.

6
What kind of help will you need?

It is no sign of incompetence to recognize the need for outside help, and, unless you are planning to engage in a very small, very localized, cash-and-carry type of business, you probably will need a lot of it. Few, if any, individuals are capable of handling the roles of butcher, baker, and candlestick maker — of serving as administrator, accountant, solicitor, personnel director, purchasing agent, tax expert, officed manager, banker, transport manager, salesman, engineer, shop foreman, and all the other functions common to running a business. Those who try to do so generally fail.

The starting point, of course, is to determine what you (and your partners, associates, and employees) can and cannot do. If you are an accountant, for example, you may not have to go outside to find one. On the other hand, you must ask yourself, How can my time be put to the best use? If you will have your hands full simply administering the business, perhaps you will not have sufficient time to handle the bookkeeping, even if you are an accountant.

Make a list of all the functions that your business requires. From the items on that list, identify the ones that you (or an associate) can do. Using that list, identify the things that you probably should not be doing. From the combination of things that you *cannot* do and the things that you *probably should not* be doing, you will have a clear picture of the areas in which you must seek help, either by adding people to your staff of by engaging someone outside the firm to handle them on a freelance or contractual basis.

The decision to add to your staff or find outside help is very easy, not unlike a manufacturer's decision to make or to buy. If the manufacturer needs a part and decides that he can get it for less by purchasing it from an outside supplier, he buys it; if he finds that he can make it for less than a supplier would charge, then he makes it himself. In the same manner, if you feel that you can purchase the help you need for less than it would cost you to add a person (or a department) to your company, then you definitely should seek help from the outside.

How do you find the kind of professional help that you need? Talk to your banker, to other business people, and to friends. Consult the *Yellow Pages*. Don't engage the first person who comes along — a person who may now live down the street, or have an office next door, or a person you were introduced to by a friend at the country club. Be as selective as you would be in choosing another employer. Ask questions. Interview every possible candidate before you make your choice.

How do you interview a professional, such as an accountant? Ask if they have had any experience handling work in your field: How many years? For what companies? See if serving your company would present any possible conflict of interest in their dealings with other clients. Discuss their services: Would they cover your needs? Discuss their fees: Are they reasonable? Do they seem interested in you, your company, and its business? Will the person you are inerviewing actually handle your business, or will it be turned over to a subordinate? Ask for references — and check them thoroughly.

Condense your starting list until you can name three or four finalists. Interview them again. Check their references again. Then make your decision.

OUTSIDERS ON THE TEAM

Simply because you have hired an outsider to handle your legal work, or accounting, or whatever, there's no reason to expect any less loyalty, commitment, confidentiality, capability, or respect than you would of an in-house employee. You are paying for the service that you get, just as you would pay an employee, and you are entitled to the person's interest, attention, suggestions, and on-time performance.

Conversely, an outsider cannot become a fully dedicated

member of your team if you do not treat him or her as such. Be sure you give outsiders all the information they need when they need it. Make yourself available to them when necessary. Let the others in your company know that the outsiders are a part of the team and should be treated as such. Plan far enough ahead to give the outsiders the proper amount of time to do their jobs. If you feel they are not performing in the manner you expect, discuss it with them and work out a solution. Encourage them to submit ideas and suggestions to improve the company. Listen to their ideas and suggestions attentively and with an open mind. If you don't understand what they are doing, or why, ask them to explain it to you. Remember, their role is to make recommendations, not decisions.

Professional expertise is often expensive. Get the most out of the situation by having meetings only when they are necessary, by keeping them short, by being prepared, by sticking to an agenda, and by getting their advice in advance, not after you're already in trouble. Learn as much as possible about what they are doing, why they are doing it, and how they are doing it, so that after a period of time you will have to have fewer meetings and ask fewer questions.

Many experienced business people now work part time for small business advice agencies. There is nothing quite like the advice of someone who has done it before. Of course, they may go about things differently from you, but they can give basic, sound business sense and flag up any potential pitfalls. The main agencies are: the Department of Employment's Small Firms Service; the Rural Development Commission and Enterprise Agencies. There are over three hundred Enterprise Agencies or Trusts in Britain. They offer not only counselling but a wide range of free or low-cost services, including workshop accommodation. You can locate your local ones either through *Yellow Pages* or by contacting Business In The Community. There are also specialist advice agencies for women, ethnic minorities and young people. The addresses of all the above are given in the appendices.

EMPLOYEES

The substance of any company is its employees. This is never more apparent than when a company is just getting started;

when it is small; when the contribution of every single employee counts.

As the boss, it will be up to you to see that each employee fulfils his or her responsibilities to the firm. You cannot allow yourself to play favourites or make exceptions. Each must do his share, and all must be treated fairly and equally.

New companies and small companies frequently employ members of the immediate family — Mum, Dad, Aunt Susan, Uncle David, sons, daughters, nieces, and nephews. The opportunities for nepotism (literally, 'favouring a nephew') generally abound. The fear of nepotism among employees who are not members of the family can be overpowering. You must deal with these concerns directly, immediately, and fairly. Employees outside the family must never be made to feel any less appreciated, less important, or less secure than anyone else.

The same considerations apply when a close friend joins the firm, or a neighbour's son or daughter. No matter who they are, what they do, or what their family connections may be, every employee must be treated with the same respect, the same concern, and the same objectivity. They all are a part of your business team.

The following working conditions are cited as most important to employees:

- Job security.
- Good wages.
- Full appreciation of their work.
- Feeling in on things.
- Interesting work.
- Good physical working conditions.
- Promotion and growth within the company.
- Tactful discipline.
- Sympathetic help with personal problems.
- Personal loyalty to workers.

The employer who keeps these concerns in mind will attract and keep good help. Employees will work harder, longer, more productively, and more happily when their company shows an interest in their well-being. Your employees' contributions to the company will continue to expand when:

- You let them know what's expected of them.
- They know what to expect of themselves.
- They know their own limitations.
- They know where and how to seek help.
- They can work without constant direction and supervision.
- They can measure their performance against a reasonable set of goals.
- They realize that rewards will follow achievement.

Good employees also can be a good source of ideas for building and improving your business. Very often, they're much closer to a troublesome situation than you are. Perhaps, through necessity, they've already learned how to solve a problem, or at least how to work around it. Perhaps their previous experience in other companies will help you to solve or avoid problems, or develop a new approach — or even a new product. As a part of your team, your employees' input can be invaluable.

Remember that the success of your company depends on the success of your employees. If you select them well, they *want* you to succeed. It would be foolish to refuse their help.

Also, remember that a valuable suggestion deserves a reward. Such rewards may be as routine as a simple 'thank you', or may be something more substantial, such as a bonus, a raise, or a promotion. The reward should suit the contribution — and is the surest way to encourage future contributions.

Those who do not accept employees' suggestions or who do not reward the ones who have made them usually discover that suggestions mysteriously stop. Such shortsightedness can lead to the ruin of your business.

More than once, we have seen, heard, or read about a situation like this: First, one or a group of employees in Company A work very hard to develop an idea that, in their opinion, will help the company's business. The management either rejects or ignores the employees' suggestion. Then the employees become disenchanted, leave Company A, and form Company B. With the experience they acquired at Company A and using the very suggestions for improvement that the management of Company A rejected, the former employees — now entrepreneurs — develop Company B into strong, aggressive, competitive organization. Company A falters, Company B prospers — and in some cases, Company B eventually dominates the market or absorbs its onetime competitor.

This scenario has a twofold moral: Find and retain good employees, and when your employees try to give you good advice, listen to them.

A BUSINESS LAWYER

Lawyers and solicitors come in a variety of sizes, shapes, and specialities. There are divorce lawyers, tax lawyers, patent lawyers, and criminal lawyers. There are general practitioners and specialists. You need to be sure that you engage one who has had training and experience in the specific aspects of the law that are necessary for the success of your business.

Again, it is wise to get the advice of others when selecting a lawyer. Ask your banker, your accountants, and other businesspeople. Interview each candidate exhaustively before you make your final selection.

The following sections look at some of the business legalities you should check carefully.

Trademarks

Before you begin to use your service mark or trademark it needs to be registered with the Trade Marks Registry which is part of the Patent Office. This will cost you about £200 per registration for each class of goods or service you want the mark to apply to. There are 34 such classes in all. Registration gives you the right to take action against anyone else using the mark. The mark has to be distinctive; like a different logo or a new word.

It takes about 15 months for the registration to be processed and you are protected during that time. The Registry will also tell you if there are any objections to your using the mark. When it is published in the *Trade Marks Journal*, someone who already has the same or a similar mark can object and you may have to start again.

To police your registered trademark, you are expected to make a reasonable effort to detect and prevent its use by others.

Others may use neither your mark nor any other mark that is 'confusingly similar' in shape, colour, wording, or overall appearance. If you discover someone else using the same or a similar mark, your solicitor should take immediate steps to resolve the conflict.

When using your mark, you should always include the TM or ® symbol to indicate that it has been registered. You may only use the mark on the products or services designated on your registration application; failure to use the mark may result in its abandonment. Overuse, on the other hand, may cause the mark to become generic, a situation that arose with 'aspirin' and came close to occurring with the use of trademarks such as 'Coke', 'Biro', and 'Xerox'.

Copyright

Everyone is aware of the protection afforded by a copyright to the author of a book or a magazine article. Less known is the right to protect a number of other things — brochures, films, even computer programs — under copyright laws. Your company may generate a great many of these works during the normal course of doing business.

As soon as a piece of work is committed to a 'tangible medium', it is protected by copyright. You do not have to register your work, but you may not sue for its infringement unless you have done so. The difficulty you face in protecting your copyright is one of proof, so keep dated copies. Furthermore, your work will pass into the public domain if you publish it without the proper copyright notice, that is, without the use of ©, 'copyright', or 'copr.'; the year when the work was first published; and the name of the copyright owner.

Although a copyright protects the manner in which a piece of work is expressed, it does not protect the idea being expressed. Anyone may use your idea, but no one may copy the manner in which you express it, as long as you have copyright protection.

Designs can be protected by registration with the Designs Registry (Patent Office). This costs about £40, plus the fee of the patent agent you use. The Registry will carry out a search for similar designs. To qualify your design must be original and *new*, so if it has been publicized it is not 'new'. Consequently you must keep the design a secret until it has been registered.

The copyright for purely functional designs lasts for your lifetime plus fifty years. A design for a 'product which appeals to the eye', registered under the Designs Act is only protected for fifteen years.

Patents

Patents are issued by the government and are a means of insuring that no one may make, sell or use your invention in this country without your permission. You cannot patent an idea, only something physical such as a product, process, material or mechanism.

To receive a patent, your invention must be novel; it must not be known or used by others already, or patented or described in a printed publication anywhere. It must involve an inventive step; not apparent to a person having ordinary skill, and be capable of industrial application, i.e., can be made or used. It must not be considered immoral. There are also some categories of ideas which are excluded, such as playing a game or a new plant variety.

To file a UK patent or a European patent (which covers all EEC countries) apply to the Patent Office in London. (See Appendix 1 for the address.) Although you can do it yourself, it is advisable to use a patent agent who should be a member of the Chartered Institute of Patent Agents or The Institute of Trade Mark Agents. Some local authorities also offer advice through business libraries or innovation centres.

The initial application fee is £10. This gives you a priority date, giving precedence over anyone else coming later with the same invention. Within one year of this you have to pay £80 for a preliminary search and examination or the application lapses. To continue after this requires a further fee of £95 and then renewal fees each year for the twenty years the patent is protected. A European patent costs about £1,500 in official fees plus national fees for each country once the patent has been granted. With Patent Agency fees, a UK patent would cost a minimum of £1,000.

PICKING THE RIGHT BANK

We have already stressed, a number of times, the importance of choosing the right bank to suit your needs. Your bank will probably become one of your closest and most valuable 'partners' in business.

How do you select the right one? Interview your bank as you would a prospective accountant. Get recommendations from your solicitor, accountant, other businesspeople, and other bankers. Visit each candidate and ask questions.

All the major banks in the UK are financially sound, but there are differences in the way that they offer services to business clients. Managers of larger branches have more discretion over lending. Some banks have special corporate branches where the staff are experienced in lending to business. All the major banks run business advisory services. Your relationship with your bank is vitally important. You have to get on with them, you have to feel you can trust them and that they will understand your business needs.

You need to know if the particular branch can handle the scale of business you intend to operate without constant referral to local directors. You also need to know if they can handle the sorts of business services you need, such as foreign currencies if you are dealing with overseas customers or suppliers. If you are dealing in cars, for example, or furniture, or major appliances, will the bank assist your customers in financing their purchases? Can the bank help you set up and administer a pension fund or profit sharing schemes or debt factoring? Some banks will even handle your payroll for you.

As you interview prospective bankers, the following chart can help you to determine how they rate. Before the interview place an X in the first column after every banking service you think your company will need. Then, as you talk with each banking representative, you will have a checklist of topics to discuss. (It's also a good idea to ask a representative number of current customers about the quality of these services.)

You may want to make photocopies of these pages so they can be reused.

Interview checklist

	Your needs	Bank 1	Bank 2	Bank 3
Commercial services				
Direct loans				
Working capital				
Overdrafts				
Term loans				
Letters of credit				
Asset-based				
Small Firms Loan Guarantee Scheme				
Lease				
Management buyout				
Advisory services				
Management succession				
Venture capital				
Performance bonds and guarantees				
Long-term capital markets				
Real estate				
Machinery, equipment				

	Your needs	Bank 1	Bank 2	Bank 3
Equity finance				
Company registration				
New issue service				

Cash management

	Your needs	Bank 1	Bank 2	Bank 3
Cash concentration/ zero balance accounts				
Factoring				
Cash reporting				
Wire transfer				
Depository transfer				

Trust

	Your needs	Bank 1	Bank 2	Bank 3
Pension				
Self-insurance				

Investments

	Your needs	Bank 1	Bank 2	Bank 3
Purchase and sales				
Collections				
Discount brokerage				
Safekeeping				
Nominee service				

	Your needs	Bank 1	Bank 2	Bank 3
Accounts				
Current				
Currency accounts				
Time deposits				
Money market				
Other				
Night drop				
Automated payroll				
Safe-deposit box				
International				
Foreign exchange				
Letters of credit				
Collections				
Acceptance financing				
Forward currency				

Personal Services

	Your needs	Bank 1	Bank 2	Bank 3
Customer loans				
Mortgage				
Personal				
Installment				
Overdrafts				
Budget accounts				

	Your needs	Bank 1	Bank 2	Bank 3
Credit cards				

Investments

	Your needs	Bank 1	Bank 2	Bank 3
Purchases and sales				
Collections				
Investment management				
Safekeeping				

Accounts

	Your needs	Bank 1	Bank 2	Bank 3
Current				
Time deposits				
Money market				
Certificates of deposit				
Ex-patriot banking				

Trust

	Your needs	Bank 1	Bank 2	Bank 3
Estate planning				
Wills				
Land trusts				
Living trusts				

Other

	Your needs	Bank 1	Bank 2	Bank 3
Taxation				
Safe-deposit box				

ADVERTISING, PROMOTION AND PUBLIC RELATIONS

Another area in which entrepreneurs often need help is in promoting their business. Too often, promotion is put to one side — perhaps when it is needed the most — simply because it is thought to be too expensive. That certainly need not be the case.

When you have company letterheads printed, that is promotion. When you design business cards, that is promotion. Putting up a sign, preparing a catalogue, having the company listed in the phone book, adopting a slogan, and creating a logo — all those things are promotion.

Promotion is a normal, necessary, and tax-deductible part of doing business. If potential customers don't hear about you, they can't give you their business. That is the purpose of promotion: to make sure they hear about you.

In general terms, the field of promotion is divided into two categories: advertising and public relations.

Advertising is the process of conveying your sales message to the public by means of a paid medium — billboards, newspapers, magazines, radio, TV, direct mail, even skywriting.

Public relations is the technique by which you convey legitimate news about your company to the public, often using the same media as those in which you might advertise. Examples of this sort of news include:

- Opening a new shop or factory.
- Announcing a new product or service.
- Changes in company management.
- Setting a new sales or safety record.
- Renovation or expansion of the shop or factory.
- Receipt of a significant contract.
- Awarding a significant contract.
- Labour negotiations.

Advertising should be considered an investment in the growth of your business. Its cost should be no more than you can reasonably afford. The media that you use should be ones that will catch the eye of your customers (or in some cases, investors).

The purpose: to generate business, to enchance the image of your firm, and to increase public awareness of your firm, its products or services, its location, or any other meaningful piece of information.

Public relations is something of a misnomer. We have many publics, not just one. They include the community in which we do business (community relations), our customers, our suppliers, our employees (employee relations), and even our local and national legislators (government relations). It is important to maintain a favourable relationship with all these publics — and one of the best ways to assure that is through communication.

Both advertising and public relations are communications techniques. In fact, many organizations group both under the broader title of marketing communications (although, as we have just pointed out, their impact frequently exceeds the area of marketing alone).

One of your first promotional concerns should be to develop and maintain a list of your customers and prospects. Whatever your field of business, this is your major public. Whenever you make a sale, add that customer to your list. Whenever someone writes in about your products or services, add their name to your list. And above all, keep your list current by promptly changing an address or the name of your contact. People are always on the move.

You can get a great deal of free promotional assistance from the advertising representatives of your local paper, Yellow Pages directory, radio station, or TV station. They will even help you to prepare your ad. Make contact, too, with journalists who write for the local papers, they need good stories and your business start is a good story isn't it?

Agencies that specialize in advertising and/or public relations may be located through the Yellow Pages. They should be interviewed and checked out with other sources — just like any other outside resource. Be particularly careful to ask about their rates and fees, because these can vary widely from agency to agency.

7
Expenses and taxes

Once you have decided what form (structure) of business you wish to have, it becomes time to set the machinery in motion.

At the very outset, we recommend three moves that we consider paramount: Get a good solicitor, get a good accountant, and make a good banking connection. Each of these will be discussed in depth later in this book.

INCOME TAXES

There is a lot of public misunderstanding about corporate taxation. Some people think that businesses do not pay enough taxes, that the tax laws allow too many corporate loopholes, and so on. What they do not realize is that, to some extent, the income generated by a corporation is taxed *twice*! Corporate profits are taxed, and then the owners (shareholders) are paid a dividend on their investment, which must be reported as income on their personal income taxes, where it is taxed again.

There are two ways to avoid this double-taxation situation.

1 If you work for the company, as a director, for example, you can draw a salary. The salary is tax deductible to the corporation, and you will pay only the individual income taxes that are due on your salary.
2 When the company is originally capitalized, you can fund it partially with shares and partially with loans to the company. While the share dividends the company gives you will be double-

taxed, the payment of interest on your loans will be tax-deductible (to the company). As an individual, of course, you will have to pay income tax on both the dividends and the interest.

Corporation tax is currently (1988/9) 25% when taxable profits do not exceed £100,000 profit, and 35% when they do (although marginal relief is applied up to profits of £500,000). An individual pays 25% on taxable income up to £19,300 but 40% thereafter. This lower tax rate for small companies allows it to retain more of its income for operating expenses and expansion. If the company is dissolved at some later time, your share of the proceeds will be taxed as a capital gain (or loss) which is also lower than the higher band of personal tax.

Companies, however, do not tend to 'liquidate' in that sense. Once formed, they tend to have a life of their own. Shares may be bought and sold; directors and officers may come and go; the company may abandon one field of endeavour and move into another; it may go bankrupt or merge with another business — but companies seldom simply stop doing business, sell off their assets, pay their bills, and distribute what's left to their shareholders.

A company may adopt a financial year that is pretty much of its own choosing. The selection of a financial year should be considered carefully because it may allow you to defer some income taxes and/or provide you with some options related to the payment of salaries or bonuses to the owners. The former might be achieved, for example, by selecting a tax year that will end after there has been a substantial amount of expense but before any substantial income has been realized. Corporation tax is normally paid nine months after the end of the financial year.

OTHER TAXES

Whether you are a sole trader, or in a partnership or limited company, you need to know something about the other taxes that you will come across.

Income tax is paid by an individual on his or her income. As an employee (perhaps as the director of your company) your salary will be liable for income tax which the company deducts on a 'pay as you earn' (PAYE) basis and remitted to the collector of taxes. As well as income tax, each employee is liable to pay National Insurance contributions. There are levels of income below which an individual pays neither income tax nor National Insurance. The Inland Revenue provide a 'pack' of information which contains full instructions and forms to deal with PAYE. Once learnt, it is a simple task to keep the wage records in order.

If you are self-employed, you are taxed annually on your profits. Your income tax is then paid in two equal instalments in January and July. However, you still have to pay your own Class 2 National Insurance contributions separately. This is explained in more detail in leaflets NI41 and NI255 from the Department of Social Security. Class 4 National Insurance, which is calculated on your profits, is collected by the Inland Revenue with your tax. The maximum you can pay under class 4 is currently £677, which is for taxable profits over £15,340, and half of this is tax deductible!

If you are going to become self-employed in the construction industry, you will need a 714 Tax Certificate, otherwise the main contractor will deduct income tax in the same way as PAYE. Also, if you are going to work as a consultant on long term contracts, you need to have proof from the Inland Revenue that you are *bona fide* self-employed, or they will expect your contractor to deduct tax as if you were an employee.

The other main day-to-day tax that many businesses have to collect and account for is value added tax or VAT. You do not need to register for VAT until your taxable turnover exceeds £22,100 per year or £7,500 a quarter. Before making any decisions on VAT you should talk to your local VAT inspector at the Customs and Excise. The VAT *General Guide (Notice 700)* contains useful, if lengthy, information. Sole traders, partnerships and limited companies are all within the scope of VAT.

Sian Brady
Installation Technology Ltd

In 1985, Sian was a technician with a major multinational company, but she was frustrated with the beauracracy and limitations of her job, which was to move computers from one place to another, ensuring that they were working properly after the move. 'I wanted to get out and do something for myself,' says Sian. She decided to start her own business and sell her expertise back to her employer and to other similar businesses. As soon as she could, she experimented with a few small jobs for other people. Over the next few months, she built up some contacts who could help her take on bigger jobs.

She found that time management and the ability to put together proposals — skills she had learnt in management services — were valuable in developing Installation Technology Ltd. She also spent some time on a training course at Durham University Business School which added commercial expertise to her existing technical expertise. She spent the next three months establishing contacts with the sorts of commercial organizations who relied on mini-computer systems and whose work was expanding into new premises.

'By thinking more strategically, I realized that my targetting and pricing could be improved. I also realized that my business needed additional capital to achieve its growth potential.' Later, Sian was to trade some equity in return for expansion.

Sian, and her partner Mark, launched the business in June 1986, having already taken a few thousand pounds worth of small jobs. In the first year, Sian received orders totalling £35,000. 'Some of the jobs were quite small to start with — just a weekend's working moving a system with half a dozen terminals,' she says.

In 1987, Installation Technology grew five-fold, reaching a turnover of £170,000. The following year it grew five-fold again, with £600,000 in the first half-year.

'I have enjoyed growing I.T., but realized I needed more management expertise within the company to grow it fast. I took on two additional directors; a senior manager from one of our big customers and an ex-finance director of a clearing bank.' The latter also took a 15 per cent share of the equity. 'Parting with equity was a big decision but has proved to be the right decision many times over,' says Sian.

Two years after the launch, their client list contains over twenty-five 'blue chip' organizations, and they are coming back for more. The order book looks like being over £2 million for the next 12 months.

Sian feels that success has come from her ability to build a first-rate complete design and installation service from a technical skill. This has meant thinking more widely, and hiring people who could do things she could not do herself.

Frustrated in a management services role, and at her lack of control in her own life, Sian Brady has found gratification, financial reward and her own form of success as an entrepreneur.

8
Where will the money come from?

Along with the legal framework of forming a business, you will need funds. Where will they come from?

Before you can make an intelligent decision about the source of capitalization, you must have an accurate assessment of the amount of capitalization you will need. You probably gave some thought to this as you prepared your business plan. Here are the basic questions:

- How thoroughly have you explored your start-up costs?
- How much will it cost to operate the business during the first year? The second year? Until the business becomes self-sustaining?
- Have you provided for the cost of additional equipment. Additional personnel? Materials and supplies? Maintenance?
- Have you provided for taxes? Licence fees? Insurance?
- How much money would it be wise to keep in reserve?
- Have you provided for your own personal economic needs? (If not from the profits of the business, then how?)

If all these factors have been weighed realistically, you will have enough idea of how much money you will need to start and operate your business. Do you have that much money on hand? If not, how much additional capital will you need — and where can you get it?

PERSONAL ASSETS

Cash in hand

How much money do you actually have available? Tally it up.
Consider what you have in your current account, savings
account, safe-deposit box, and in various cash-convertible securities, such as shares savings certificates.

Some people have put a little money away over a span of years
so that, someday, they may be able to own their own business.
A friend of mine calls it his 'I quit' money.

Other assets

Do you have shares, debentures or securities that you'd be willing to sell? A car or a boat that isn't needed? Do you have other
property that you would sell, such as a holiday home, or perhaps
a coin, stamp, book, or art collection? Would you consider
remortgaging your house or some other form of property? Can
you take out a loan against your life insurance or the life insurance of your spouse or children? Does anyone owe you money
that can be collected? If you are currently employed by another
company, will you receive an early retirement settlement, a pension settlement, or a termination settlement? Are you entitled
to a year-end bonus or some other form of extra compensation?

FRIENDS AND RELATIVES

Do you have any friends and relatives who would be interested
in investing in the business — or who could be persuaded to
make you (or the business) a loan?

PARTNERS AND ASSOCIATES

How much money will the company be able to raise from those
who will be participating in the business with you, such as partners, shareholders, or employees?

DEBT FINANCING

Having exhausted the sources of capital most directly available to you and your business associates (if any), you will have to look elsewhere for additional money that may be needed. This may be the first real test of your business acumen.

Potential lenders will be interested primarily in two things: Will you and your business be able to generate sufficient earnings to repay the debt? Do you, or the business, have any collateral to further assure repayment of the debt?

The nature and financial posture of the business will determine what type of financing may be obtained, as well as the source(s) of that type of financing. Good financial documentation will be essential, as will a well-developed business plan. The manner in which you state your case when seeking financial assistance goes a long way towards convincing lenders that you have the managerial ability to run your business effectively (and hence earn enough money to repay their loan). It may even be wise to get help from a lawyer and an accountant when you prepare your documentation and when you make your presentation to a prospective lender. This quiz will be very helpful.

Your self-evaluation as a financial risk

Are you a good financial risk?

Why do you need the money?
To expand the business	10 points
To operate the business	5 points
To start a business	0 points

How long have you been in business?
Three years or more	10 points
One to three years	5 points
Just beginning	0 points

Does the business have a good financial history and good prospects for continued profitability?
Strong history/outlook	10 points
Steady history/outlook	5 points

*Inconsistent history, no history, history of losses, or poor
outlook*   0 points

What is the business's profitability and return on
investment compared to the industry average?
Above average   10 points
Average   5 points
Below average   0 points

Divide the business's current assets by its current liabilities.
How does this ratio compare to the industry average?
Above average   10 points
Average   5 points
Below average   0 points

Do you have established banking or funding sources?
Several   10 points
My local bank   5 points
No   0 points

Are you well-known in the community?
Widely known   10 points
Somewhat known   5 points
No   0 points

How are your personal and business credit ratings?
Good to excellent   10 points
Fair   5 points
Poor or unrated   0 points

Do you have a business plan?
Formally prepared and documented   10 points
Informally prepared and/or documented   5 points
No   0 points

How are your controls over finances and internal accounting?
Good to excellent   10 points
Weak in some areas   5 points
Poor or nonexistent   0 points

Do you have sufficient business insurance?
Yes, including 'key man' insurance   10 points
Generally good   5 points
No   0 points

Considering administration, policy, marketing, finance, personnel, and production as the key functions in your business, how many do you handle yourself?

Two	10 points
Three or four	5 points
Five or all	0 points

How would someone evaluate your employees' competence, experience, and loyalty?

Above average	10 points
Average	5 points
Below average	0 points

Total points   _____

Remember that this is a self-evaluation test. Lenders, who are typically and traditionally conservative, may be less kind. Still, *if you score 100 points or more* on this analysis, you should be able to get the funds that you need at a reasonable cost. *If you score between 50 and 100*, it will help to have good connections with the lender. Can you improve in any of the areas above in which you scored poorly? *If your score is below 50*, you'll definitely have some problems locating funds.

COMMERCIAL BANKS

The most common source of business funding is the commercial bank, and, for that reason, it is wise to select your company's bank wisely and carefully. Obviously, the bank with which you do business on a daily basis is more likely to sympathize with your need for funds than some other bank. It will also know a great deal more about your financial situation than another bank; that is, your average daily bank balance, your cash flow position, your credit rating, and so forth.

It is also important to select a bank that knows your community and/or knows something about the industry in which you are doing business. The more knowledgeable they are, the more likely they will be to look upon your situation realistically — and favourably.

Your bank should become one of your key business partners. Try to affiliate with one that will serve not only the needs of your business but those of your employees and customers, and one that is capable of offering special services, such as import/ export assistance or cash management. Review the quality and character of the bank's management carefully. Read their reports. Talk to their current customers. Compare thoroughly before you decide.

The choice of banks for most new businesses usually rests between the major high street banks, giving a choice of perhaps five or six in any one locality, although there are in fact over twenty 'clearing and domestic deposit' banks. The size of a branch that you deal with may be important. Often the manager of a large branch can lend more without having to obtain the permission of a regional head office. This can be important, because you will want to build up a good relationship with your regular manager, not wait for someone else to make a decision.

The banks offer a very wide range of services to business clients as well as a variety of financing packages. The most common types of loan for small business are the normal overdraft facility for working capital and medium-term loans for assets and working capital. The banks also offer, either directly or through subsidiaries, leasing, factoring, discounting, export finance, hire purchase and even equity capital.

You can expect to pay the base rate plus one to four (percentage) points for a business loan. If you are starting a new business, the bank — like most other sources of funding — will probably want some personal guarantee as security and as proof of your commitment to the business.

Incidentally, never get the idea that a lender is doing you a favour. No banking institution that I know of will do you or anyone else a favour. Lending is their business — and most of them are quite good at it.

Bankers believe that a business is an extension of its principals. If you know your field and use good financial controls, you probably will be viewed as a good risk.

MERCHANT BANKS
(ACCEPTANCE HOUSES)

These specialize in the financing services which the clearing banks offer as part of their wide range. Generally speaking, they are not interested in amounts of less than £50,000. The address of the Accepting Houses Committee is given in Appendix 1. Typical houses are Guinness Mahon & Co. Ltd, Lazard Brothers & Co. Ltd, and Morgan Grenfell & Co. Ltd.

FINANCE HOUSES

Finance houses provide short-term credit. Typically, this would be a hire-purchase agreement with repayments by instalments over a period of two to five years. There are a large number of finance houses and they are very active in the financing of fixed assets for small business. The address of their association is given in Appendix 1.

FACTORING

Factoring your invoices or your complete sales ledger is a common way of funding working capital requirements. The principle is that as soon as you sell something on credit to a customer, the factoring company pays you a large proportion of the invoice value. They then wait for the customer to settle the debt, then you are paid the rest, less the commission. This is a particularly useful way of financing rapid growth. Some factoring companies take over the complete debt management, they send out invoices and statements and they collect the debts for you. The charge for the service depends on the number and average size of invoices and is between 0.75 and 3 per cent of turnover. The interest rate charged is similar to bank overdraft rates. The main disadvantage is that you cannot then use your debtors as an asset to secure your bank overdraft, but you shouldn't need so much anyway.

The advantage is that you can obtain needed capital without increasing your debt or reducing your equity in the company. You may also experience:

- Increased liquidity.
- Reduced overhead.
- Greater operating efficiency.
- Better planning capability.
- Improved customer relations.
- Improved buying relations.
- More opportunities to optimize your sales potential.
- More opportunities for early payment discounts.
- More opportunities to make large volume purchases.
- Being able to limit your ratio of credit and collection expense to credit sales.

ASSET-BASED LENDING

Most lending to small firms is secured. Usually lenders will want some physical security plus guarantees. It is as well to resist their demands for personal guarantees and for the use of private assets, such as your house, as security. Lenders will argue that you must show commitment. However if their IOUs are fully secured, they might not be so committed to your success. There are times in the life of every small firm when the going gets very rough and commitment by your bankers is the only thing that gets you through, so you should strive to reduce your personal liability to as little as possible while motivating the bank to back you wholeheartedly. Usually the compromise is to guarantee only a specific maximum limit.

The ideal situation is for the firm to be its own guarantor, where loans are underwritten by 'charges' on the assets of the business. These loans are called debentures. The charge may be on a specific asset, such as a machine or stock or 'floating' on the value of all the assets. Most lenders look for 'a fixed and floating charge', i.e., they back both horses in a two horse race.'

When assets are valued for the purposes of underwriting a loan, the value is usually some way below 'market' rates. The reason is that if the assets ever had to be sold to repay the loan, it would be in difficult circumstances and also in a hurry. Such a sale attracts lower prices, also market rates tend to fluctuate. Typically a house will be valued at 70 per cent of its value (less, of course, any mortgage outstanding). Debtors would be valued at between 70 to 90 per cent, stock at anywhere from 15 to 75 per cent.

THE SMALL FIRMS LOAN GUARANTEE SCHEME

If you have millions of pounds, then borrowing millions more doesn't seem to be too difficult, and the interest rates are very near base rate. However if you want the bank to lend you twenty or thirty thousand, they want guarantees and also charge relatively high rates. The Loan Guarantee Scheme is an attempt to improve this situation while letting the 'market' operate normally. The government provides the bank with a guarantee for each small business loan made under the scheme. The guarantee should only apply when the borrower has already pledged personal assets to support ordinary bank lending. Any assets which the business owns must be pledged as security for the loan. On this basis the government will guarantee to the bank 70 per cent of the total loan in return for a 2.5 per cent interest premium paid quarterly by the borrower to the government. The loan can be up to £75,000 over a period of two to seven years. Some banks have a minimum of £15,000. The scheme is worthwhile when your security is fully utilized but you have a good commercial proposition. The total cost is around 4 per cent over base rate.

LEASING COMPANIES

Leasing may not be a way to acquire capital, but it is a way to acquire the things that capital would buy if you had it. Therefore, by means of leasing, you finance your business on someone else's money, in a manner of speaking.

Actually, leasing is a form of secured lending. It is commonly used to finance vehicles, construction and other heavy equipment, office machines and furniture, computers, and real estate. Since the lessor retains the title to the property you are leasing, you — the lessee — are able to 'finance' virtually the entire cost.

For a new company, leasing may offer a great many benefits. Among them are that:

- Leasing companies usually are unconcerned about how long you have been in business, what your business projections may be, and so on.
- You will need little or no cash up front.
- Leases are fully tax-deductible.
- Leases frequently run for a longer term than a loan of similar amount, which often means that your monthly payments will be lower.
- Leasing is available even in times of tight money, when cash loans may be hard to get.
- Leasing on an installment plan, you may be able to acquire more equipment than you could afford to buy, or you may be able to acquire the needed equipment sooner than if you had to wait until the company could afford to buy it.
- Some items may be scarce and require a considerable waiting period from order to delivery. Leasing companies may be able to give you immediate delivery.
- You may be hesitant to buy certain things out of concern that they will soon become obsolete, such as rapidly changing technologies like data processing or telecommunications equipment. When you lease such equipment, you usually can exchange it for more advanced equipment as it becomes available.

Several variations offer tax-sheltered advantages to investors. A common one calls for a group of investors to purchase or construct a depreciable asset specifically for the purpose of leasing it to your business. Another is the *sale-lease back transaction*, in which the business sells a depreciable asset to a group of investors and then leases it back from them. The company receives the sale price of the asset and probably recaptures some depreciation, while the new owners receive enough rental income to cover the cost of refinancing the property, if necessary, plus the benefit of a faster depreciation rate, allowed on newly acquired assets.

SUPPLIERS

Suppliers who provide materials, products, or services on credit are helping you finance your business. When the supplier sends you £5,000 worth of goods, it is the equivalent of lending you £5,000 for thirty, sixty, or ninety days (depending on the terms of your credit agreement). If you pay for the goods within the specified period of time, the effect is the same as having received an interest-free loan.

Let's look at an example. Assume that you are opening a clothing shop, that a manufacturer ships you £5,000 worth of clothing, and that payment is due within thirty days. Also assume that you use a 50 per cent markup, that you sell the entire shipment quickly, and that you pay the manufacturer within the specified thirty days.

First, you will have had the use of the manufacturer's £5,000, albeit in goods, for thirty days interest-free.

Second, you will have realized a gross profit (before overhead and taxes) of £2,500 from the use of that money (£5,000 times 50 per cent).

Third, you will have strengthened your relationship with the manufacturer so that, in future dealings, that supplier will be more likely to advance you an even greater amount of merchandise on credit and/or allow you a longer period of time in which to pay your bill (sixty or ninety days, perhaps, rather than thirty).

Obviously, such relationships are valuable and should be treated as such. A good relationship with your supplier can result in a larger line of credit and more liberal credit terms, but a bad relationship can do just the opposite.

Phil and Janet McKenna
McKenna Heat Treatment Ltd.

Phil McKenna was a technologist with over ten years' experience in the heat treatment of metals. At the age of 30, with his career going nowhere, he decided to set up his own business for metal heat treatment. He worked day and night perfecting his business plan to establish this company and in mid 1985 he launched his business. Almost immediately Phil won a major business award for the most promising start up, an award which included cash, premises and free consultancy advice.

The only two things Phil didn't have at that point were money and customers, but he knew they were out there and would soon be flocking to him in droves. 'What we now know,' says his partner, Janet, 'is that you really have to plan well in advance and that customers take a long time to change their habits. Plenty of people would be better off buying from us, but they take a long time to realize that.'

Despite their slow start and the fact that they now had no money to 'match' that of outside finance, the McKennas were backable. Early in 1986, their financial advisers helped them to put together a sound financing plan which would give them enough time to build up the business.

Their £105,000 of assets and the £50,000 they needed in working capital were funded by £20,000 of their own money by remortgaging their house, £55,000 of shares bought by a venture capital company for 33% of the equity, £30,000 of long term loan from British Coal Enterprises, equipment leasing of £20,000 and an overdraft facility of £30,000.

In 1987 they turned over £110,000 and made a smaller loss than expected. In 1988 they are hitting sales of £30,000+ per month and those slow-to-change customers are gradually becoming the regular customers of McKenna Heat Treatment Ltd.

Table 5
Sources of debt funding

Loan types	Clearing banks	Accepting houses	Factoring companies	Finance houses	Development and venture capital institutions
Demand					
Short term (3 years or less)	Frequent	Occasional	Frequent	Frequent	Rare
Intermediate (3—15 years)	Occasionally up to 10 years	Frequent	Rare	Occasionally up to 10 years	Frequent
Long term	Rare	Occasional	Rare	Rare	Occasional

Loan types	Clearing banks	Accepting houses	Factoring companies	Finance houses	Development and venture capital institutions
Revolving credit (i.e., overdraft)	Frequent	Occasional	Frequent	Rare	Occasional
Uses Working capital	Frequent	Frequent	Frequent	Occasional	Occasional
Growth capital machinery and equipment	Frequent	Occasional	Rare	Frequent	Occasional
Premises	Rare	Occasional	Never	Rare	Frequent
Acquisitions or general expansion	Frequently	Frequently	Rare	Rare	Frequent
Risk capital	Rare	Rare	Never	Never	Frequently
Amounts available	Varies by collateral and need	Not often less than 50,000	up to 80% of invoice or debtors	up to 100% of new asset	Varies considerably by provider
Interest rate	Base rate plus 2 to 6 points depending on type of loan and risk involved	Base rate plus 2 to 6 points depending on type of loan and risk involved	Base rate plus 2 to 4 points plus management fee of 0.75% to 3% of turnover	True rates are almost double 'flat' rates quoted. Often 10 points above base	Wide range depending on provider
Guarantees and security required	Frequently, though not always	Frequent	Credit limits and insurance of debtors	Retain title of asset	Frequent
Financial statements	Audited preferred	Audited	Audited preferred	Audited preferred	Audited
Request documents	Up to date accounts and cashflow forecast, plus simple business plan	Accounts plus business proposal for larger amounts	Not complex, current debtors list and payment record	Usually simple. Purchase of uncommon equipment may require appraisal	Thorough business plan usually required. Large scale packages can become complex

Loan types	Clearing banks	Accepting houses	Factoring companies	Finance houses	Development and venture capital institutions
Borrower stage of development					
Start-up	Frequent	Occasional	Occasional	Frequent	Occasional
Growth	Frequent	Frequent	Frequent	Frequent	Frequent
Maturity	Preferred	Preferred	Occasional	Frequent	Occasional

SMALL BUSINESS FINANCE SCHEMES

There are over a hundred schemes run by the government, local authorities, charities, enterprise agencies, etc., which provide financial support for small businesses. They are usually offered as an incentive to people to do what they otherwise would not have done. For example, the government's Regional Enterprise Grants and Regional Selective Assistance are offered to certain types of businesses when they start up, expand or relocate in a Development Area (Development Areas are economically depressed).

These grants are well worth seeking. They can run into tens of thousands of pounds and do not have to be repaid. Normally such grants are obtained from the Department of Trade and Industry (DTI), who also provide a number of consultancy grants for business improvement. There are development agencies in Scotland, Wales and Northern Ireland who have their own incentive schemes to encourage investment and new business.

Some grants are only given on the grounds that without them the project would not go ahead or would not happen so quickly. The implication of this 'additionality' criterion is that you cannot apply for the grants after making the expenditure or commitment. You must get approval of the grant *before* going ahead with the project.

An incentive to encourage people to try self-employment is the Department of Employment's Enterprise Allowance Scheme. This is offered to unemployed people who are starting up a business in which they will be employed full time. The grant is £40 per week for one year.

There are a number of schemes to encourage young people into business. Finance is offered alongside counselling support, so that the young people receive guidance as well as cash. The Prince's Youth Business Trust makes a major contribution to young enterprise in the form of grants and loans up to several thousand pounds. There are also a number of competitions, for example Livewire, which each year offers over £100,000 in prize money each year to entrepreneurs under the age of 25.

The finance scene is constantly changing, so you must seek professional advice, especially if the amounts are significant to you. The availability of grants and special loans in your locality will be well known to your local Enterprise Agency or Trust, the Department of Employment's Small Firms Centres and the regional offices of the Department of Trade and Industry. The Industrial Development Office of your local authority should also prove a good source of information. Some useful names and addresses are given in the appendices.

The availability of a grant or loan should *never* be the justification for going into business. You must have a sound proposition, based on the true costs of the business. Too many people start up and do not cost in their wages, because they are receiving aid, or rent because they have been offered rent-free accommodation in the short term. If the business is viable at full costs, then go for it and take advantage of any incentives you can.

EQUITY FUNDING

Up to now, we have been talking about ways to raise funds without having to sacrifice any of your equity (ownership) in the business. Sometimes that is sufficient, but in other circumstances, you may find that 'selling' a part of the business is the only way to get the capital you need.

When a corporation sells shares, it is selling equity. There are a number of ways equity may be used to raise capital. (It has been shown that high-tech companies that encourage their workers to own shares have grown 275 per cent faster that those whose share ownership is limited to only their top officials.)

Wealthy individual investors

Many wealthy individuals enjoy — and profit from — helping new businesses get started. They may have a special interest in the business or technology that is involved. They may be flattered by an offer to sit on your Board of Directors. They may have a relative or friend who is looking for a job.

The business skills and contacts these individuals may make available to your company may be as important as their investment.

Such benefactors generally do not want to take an active part in the management or operation of the company. They often do not have predetermined standards by which they measure a potential investment. They may expect a 300 to 500 per cent return on their investment within a relatively short time, however, and tax benefits are often extremely important to them.

Some may be willing to guarantee a business loan, even if they do not invest in the company directly.

Look for personal friends, friends of friends, or friends of business associates. Approach previous employers. See if there are those whose businesses would stand to benefit along with yours — a supplier or a potential customer, for example.

The Business Expansion Scheme (BES) can make such investments highly tax-efficient. Within the scope of the scheme, the money used for equity financing of small businesses can be untaxed as income. So if your wealthy friend earns £50,000 a year and invests £10,000 in your business, then she or he may not be taxed on that £10,000 of income. There are, of course, many rules governing the BES, one of which is that the funds must be used to purchase ordinary shares in a limited company, so partnerships and sole proprietorships are out. Negotiations with both investor and the Inland Revenue can take up to nine months, so you cannot do things in a hurry.

As well as your own business contacts and your accountant, there are several more formal ways of finding wealthy individuals to invest in your business idea. LINC, the Local Investment Networking Company is run by some Enterprise Agencies. The bulletin they send out lists business ideas looking for backers. The agencies do a preliminary feasibility study on the proposal and organize presentations at investors' meetings. Nothing is guaranteed. *Venture Capital Report* is a publication in which business proposals are advertised to prospective investors. Details of these two organizations are given in Appendix 1.

You might also find investors advertising in the business sections of quality newspapers. If you plan to advertise your own business to investors, you must take legal advice. For example, if you publish a prospectus then you need a stockbroker or similar adviser and you need to be a public limited company.

Some investors prefer to use special Business Expansion Scheme funds set up by fund management companies. Such funds tend to favour asset-based investments and are a relatively expensive way of raising finance because of arrangement fees and the need to pay non-executive directors appointed by the fund managers. Schemes are advertised in the financial newspapers and journals, and will be known to good small business advisers.

Venture capital

Venture capitalists are primarily interested in firms with an exceptional growth potential. They acquire a minority interest in the firm, sometimes provide management assistance, and expect their profits to stem from the appreciation of their equity and from capital gains tax benefits.

Venture capital may be sought from several sources:

- Investment companies specializing in this type of financing.
- Large industrial companies.
- Insurance companies.
- Trust funds.
- Banks.
- Regional development agencies.
- Pension Funds.

For venture capitalists, the quality of the company's management team, the industry involved, and the merit of the company's products or services are usually of paramount importance. They generally prefer to invest in companies from two to four years old, with capitalization of about £500,000, and with annual revenues between £1 million and £5 million. The companies in which they invest often tend to show a very small net profit or even a loss. Venture capitalists are rarely interested in making an investment of less than £100,000. They want a 20 to 60 per cent compounded rate of return on their investments each year, depending on the risk involved.

There are some venture and development capital institutions who will invest in smaller firms with growth potential. The industry estimates that the cost of making an investment is around £25,000, whether the sum invested is £5,000 or £500,000. So it's easy to see why small deals are out of favour. Often the financial package will be a mixture of loans and equity. Although they put in most of the cash, the investor will still only take a minority shareholding, usually only up to 30 per cent. This leaves room for further investors to come in when the company needs more finance, but gives the investor minority voting rights.

Venture capitalists are also interested in the *liquidity* of their investment , i.e., their ability to convert their securities back into cash whenever they choose to do so. Therefore, they prefer to invest in a company that is on the threshold either of going public or of being acquired by a publicly held company.

Venture capitalists strive to earn a return of some 500 per cent on their investments within three years, or 1000 per cent within five years. To understand how much equity you might be expected to exchange in order to obtain their financing, it is best to study an example.

Assume your projected third-year earnings will be £3 million, and assume that similar publicly held corporations are selling shares at ten times their annual earnings. Venture capitalists will then value your firm at £30 million (£3 million times 10). If they are willing to invest £3 million in your company, they will want that investment to be worth £15 million in three years (£3 million times 500 per cent). Therefore, venture capitalists will expect half the company's stock (£15 million divided by £30 million) in exchange for their investment.

Although they generally prefer to take a passive role in the management of a business, leaving it to you to direct its growth, venture capitalists will react quickly and energetically if the business does not perform according to expectations and will insist that specific changes be made where needed.

To protect their equity position, venture capitalists frequently make certain demands, which may include controls on:

- Directors' salaries.
- The company's borrowing powers.
- Alterations to share capital.
- The sale or transfer of the company.
- Directors' other interests.

Realistically, one should look upon venture capitalists as partners rather than as simple investors. They can provide your business with a great many services as you make the complex transition from a closely held organization to one that is going public. Venture capitalists also have many valuable contacts and a great deal of business experience to put at your disposal. Their advice and assistance might well be crucial to your company's success.

There are well over ninety venture capital funds. A list, showing their investment size and other criteria can be obtained from the British Venture Capital Association (address is in Appendix 1).

Going public

Although principally for more mature businesses, the public market has been known to allow younger businesses to make early initial public offerings, particularly when they seem to offer exceptionally high growth potential.

Going public is the eventual goal of many entrepreneurs, and there are a number of advantages to doing so, such as:

- Offering the company's founders, who may have invested a lot of their personal assets to finance the start-up of the firm, a greater degree of liquidity.
- Reducing the original shareholders' risk by further diversifying the company's ownership.
- Ongoing access to the market to meet future funding requirements.
- Use of the securities for purposes of acquisition.
- Use of the securities to attract key personnel or as a management incentive.
- Increased company prestige.

- Increased public awareness of the business (suppliers, customers, employees, *et al*).

There are some offsetting disadvantages to going public. They might include

- High initial cost.
- The ongoing cost of complying with regulations.
- Constant pressure to pay dividends and increase the rate of earnings.
- Restrictions on insider transactions, both with the business and with its securities.
- A loss of confidentiality.
- Potential acquisition.

The cost of a full listing on the Stock Exchange is high — a minimum of £200,000 plus ongoing expensive commitments in terms of auditing and publicity. The more usual form of entry into public markets for a growing business is to join the Unlisted Securities Market (USM) or the Over The Counter Market. The costs of these are less — about 10 per cent of the finance raised — but the expectations of growth and profit are high. Going public is something you do when you are ambitious, well in control and able to use other people's money better than they can themselves.

What do potential investors expect when they buy shares in a new company?

- A company with a well-developed product and good marketing capability.
- Some sort of leadership in its field.
- Annual growth potential of 30 to 50 per cent.
- Current sales of £5 million.
- Current profits of £250,000.

If these elements do not exist, it might be wiser to find your finance elsewhere. The question of whether you should go public or not involves a great many factors.

- Do you need money to support growth, buy equipment, engage in research and development, or pay back debt? And do you wish to do it without adding to the burden of debt?

- Do you wish to increase the public's awareness of your firm and its products?
- Do you want a way to get future financing more readily?
- Do you want to regain some of your investment in the company?
- Do you want to be able to attract and retain better employees?

Any of these is a good reason for taking your company public. A publicly traded company offers investors a security (share ownership) which can be traded freely and which has a more determinable market value. Once it has been taken public, the company's net worth may increase, its debt to equity ration will probably improve, giving more borrowing power, and it can use its shares instead of cash to pay for acquisitions. Public flotations have made many owner-managers into millionaires.

Shares can be floated on the USM in three ways. A *placement* is where sponsors place the shares to be sold with appropriate private or institutional investors. An *offer for sale* is where the shares are offered to the public, with underwriters taking up any shares which the public fail to purchase. An *introduction* is where there are already a number of public shareholders and the company does not want to sell any more new shares.

An alternative to the Stock Exchange is the Over the Counter Market run by the investment bankers MJH Nightingale & Company. This offers the advantages of making shares publicly available without the attendant high costs of going public. Nightingale's manage the buying and selling orders, acting as agents rather than principals.

THE TOOLS FOR RAISING FUNDS

Having explored the various sources of funding, we should examine the various instruments that may be required.

Once again, we must make the distinction between debt and equity funding.

Debt financing is favoured by companies because their payments on debt are tax deductible, because it requires no sacrifice of equity (ownership) in the company, and because they may derive some leverage opportunities with that sort of financing. It is favoured by investors because it provides a fixed income and because it provides the most protection for their investment, since holders of debt securities usually have top priority in the event of liquidation or reorganization.

Equity financing is favoured by companies because they are not committed to a fixed rate of repayment, because they must make dividend payments only if sufficient income is available, and because it's often an easier way to raise capital when a company is new and does not have an established record of profitability. It is favoured by investors who have a great deal of confidence in the company and expect to benefit from its growth in two ways: their dividends plus an appreciation in the value of their equity.

Medium- to long-term debt financing involves instruments such as mortages, debentures, conversion rights and guarantees.

The mortgage is a very familiar instrument. The loan, over 2 to 30 years, is made on the security of an asset, usually a house or building. The interest rate may be fixed, but more often is linked to the variations in the LIBOR (London Inter-Bank Offered Rate). The rate will usually be 3 to 5 points over base rate.

The debenture is a transferable loan made to private or public limited companies. The debenture is secured on the assets of the company (either fixed to a specific asset or on a floating charge on all the assets). The ownership of the loan can be transferred from one holder to another. For smaller companies, the debenture holder will be one lender, such as the bank. The holder of a debenture has top priority among lenders for payment if the firm fails. Larger companies offer debenture stock, which gives many lenders the opportunity to share the loan. Because a debenture is more secure, the interest rates are normally less than for an unsecured loan.

With the provision of special small business loans by all the main clearing banks and the introduction of the Small Firms Loan Guarantee Scheme, the use of debentures for smaller firms has reduced.

Convertable options which allow loans to be converted into shares are becoming more common, even at the smaller end of the market. For example, a subsidiary of the National Westminster bank currently offers something called the Capital Loan Scheme. This provides a term loan on fixed interest rates and gives the lender the option to subscribe for up to 25 per cent of the company's equity at any time during the loan repayment period. The loan ranks for repayment after creditors and before directors' and shareholders' loans. The loan is unsecured, but some limited guarantees are required from directors.

Equity financing usually involves either ordinary shares or preference shares.

Ordinary shares are the owners' capital. The shares are rewarded by dividends only after all other costs have been met. They stand last in line for any surplus if the company is wound up. Normally they carry voting rights. Two subclasses of ordinary shares are *deferred ordinary shares*, which rank after ordinary shares and *preferred ordinary shares* which rank before ordinary shares.

Preference shares give their holders rights over holders of the ordinary shares. Preference shares are normally rewarded at a fixed rate of dividend, but unlike loans, cannot be repaid except on the winding up of the company. *Participating preference shares* entitle their holders to further participation in the share of profits.

Both classes of preference shares rank before ordinary shares, but after loans, in their rights over the assets of the company. Preference shares may also be *cumulative*; when interest due but unpaid accumulates from year to year, *redeemable*; where the shares can be realized; or *convertible*, when they can be converted into ordinary shares.

Table 6

Sources of Equity Funding

	Wealthy individuals	*Venture capital (Institutional risk takers)*	*Unlisted Securities Market*	*Full Stock Market*
Frequent uses	Start-ups or early growth	Start-up (speciality sources) or growth (pre-public by 3-7 years)	Fast growing 3-10 years old or demerged from larger firms (buy-outs)	Mature or very high growth businesses

	Wealthy individuals	Venture capital (Institutional risk takers)	Unlisted Securities Market	Full Stock Market
Devices — structure preferred	Ordinary shares and secured loans	Combination of equity (ordinary and preference) and debt (debentures and convertible loans)	Ordinary shares Preference shares and loan stock (debentures)	Ordinary shares Preference shares and loan stock (debentures)
Amounts generally available	Varies by individual	From £5,000 upwards, but usually in range £50,000 to £1m.	Usual range of £1m to £10m capitalization	Over £5m capitalization
Cost	Varies; criteria are not formal; regular interest payments or dividends are often expected	High capital growth sought a compound rate of 20% to 60% per annum over 5 years, after which the investor would want a flotation or sale to realize the profit	5% to 10% of money raised. Ongoing costs thereafter include compliance costs, dividend payments and capital growth expectations.	£200,000 is minimum cost. After which, high compliance costs and regular dividend payments as well as capital growth expectations
Ownership required	Significant minority position 50/50 or 60/40 are common. A Business Expansion Scheme investor can hold a maximum of 30%.	Minority position preferred (up to 40%) Contract may give them option to majority share purchase	Only 10% of total equity need be made available to public	Minimum of 25% of total equity must be made publicly available
Documentation	Informal, except for negotiations with the Revenue on BES tax relief	Formal and extensive business plans and implementing procedures	Prospectus and an independent report must be available to investors	Expensive and formal; full prospectus has to be published in national newspapers
Financial Statements	Audited preferred	Audited	Audited	Audited

	Wealthy individuals	Venture capital (Institutional risk takers)	Unlisted Securities Market	Full Stock Market
Other	Active management involvement or on Board; personal tax considerations are important	Passive or active management often through Board membership and ongoing monitoring. Can offer significant management assistance	Participation varies, depending on ownership. Institutional investors may require non-executive directorships	Significant continuing responsibilities and control influences by Stock Market and government
Preferred or principal method of contract	Direct by referral	Referral or intermediate journal	Direct placement with investor or offer for sale or an introduction via stockbrokers and underwriters	Investment bankers, stockbrokers and underwriters

STARTING INTO BUSINESS: A CHECKLIST

By now, most of your organizational, funding, and staffing options have been studied and, hopefully, decided. Just to make sure everything has been covered, you should examine the following checklist.

Business structure
1 Sole proprietor
2 Partnership
3 Company
  (a) Articles and Memorandum
  (b) Board of Directors
  (c) Officers
  (d) Determination of financial year
  (e) Issue of shares

Initial funding

1 Personal funds
2 Family
3 Friends
4 Business associates
5 Other sources
  (a) Clearing bank
  (b) Merchant bank
  (c) Development funds
  (d) Finance house
  (e) Factoring company
6 Government funds
  (a) Regional Selective Assistance
  (b) Regional Enterprise grants
  (c) Research and development grants
  (d) Consultancy grants
  (e) Enterprise allowance
7 Equity funding
  (a) Individual investors
  (b) Business Expansion Scheme funds
  (c) Venture capital firm
  (d) Public securities markets
Other

Staff

1 In-house personnel
2 Outside
  (a) Accountant
  (b) Bankers
  (c) Commercial solicitor
  (d) Enterprise Agency
  (e) Small Firms Service counsellor
  (f) Advertising and public relations

Business site, building or office space

1 Rented
2 Purchased
3 Constructed

Documentation

1 Business plan
2 Financial plan

3 Promotion plan
4 Certificate of Incorporation or partnership agreement
5 Local authority licences
6 VAT and PAYE guides and registration if necessary
7 Trademark or service mark registration
8 Insurance cover
9 Other

Yourself

1 Motivation and commitment to make it succeed
2 Support from your family
3 Training for technical skills
4 Training for business skills
5 Knowledge of your customers and other contacts

If there are any loose ends, this is the time to take care of them. Having your organizational, funding, and staffing work completed before you go into business will enable you to devote your total energy to running the company and guiding it to a successful beginning. Typically, that will keep you as busy as you'll care to be for a number of years.

Part III

Running the business

9
Plan your business

You've taken the plunge and started a business. As the boss, the responsibility for its success or failure rests mainly on you. As the sign on Harry Truman's desk read, 'The buck stops here.'
As the head of the firm, it is now up to you to:

- Create a strategy and plan for the company's long-term development.
- Establish a short-term objective to enable it to fulfil the plan.
- Set up policies to assure consistency.
- Use your assets — money, materials and equipment — for maximum efficiency and minimum waste.
- Develop human resources to assure growth.

You must perform as an effective leader by:

- Delegating authority and responsibility.
- Providing a reasonable amount of autonomy for key people.
- Establishing a success-orientated working environment.
- Monitoring the progress of employees.
- Providing challenging, motivating, and stimulating goals.
- Helping employees to develop — personally, professionally, technically, and economically.
- Creating an atmosphere in which your company will sustain and thrive, even after you leave.

SETTING GOALS AND OBJECTIVES

Every organization should have two sets of goals and objectives. The major (long-term) set is the one that has been written into your business plan. The second (short-term) set helps to direct the organization towards its long-range objectives and keeps it from wandering too far afield.

This is not to say that your basic business plan should be so restrictive that it does not provide room for growth or new opportunities. Far from it. In fact, one should review the business plan periodically to see if the economy, the market place, the various competitive influences within the industry, and any other factors that may have existed several months or years ago have changed, thereby suggesting new directions for the company's business strategy.

Dwight Eisenhower directed the largest, most complex planning operation in history — the D-Day invasion. Yet Eisenhower fully realized, as he once remarked, that 'planning is essential, but plans are useless.' In other words, plans aren't worth anything unless and until they are converted into action that brings about the desired result.

Six basic steps are involved in effective planning.

1 Defining goals
   (a) Be brief
   (b) Put them in writing
   (c) Be specific
   (d) Be sure they're measurable
2 Collecting all relevant data
   (a) Consider the best methods
   (b) Take changed circumstances or conditions into account
3 Selecting the best method
   (a) Eliminate unnecessary steps
   (b) Simplify
   (c) Determine priorities
4 Developing the plan
   (a) Select and train people
   (b) Provide the necessary resources

    (c)   Eliminate the obstacles
5 Implementing the plan
    (a)   Revise as necessary
6 Following up
    (a)   Be persistent

But plans are only guidelines to helping you reach a specific goal. And to do that, they must be relevant, understandable, measurable, behavioural (i.e., acceptable to those who must actually carry them out), and achievable.

SOME COMMON START-UP PROBLEMS

It would be impossible to anticipate and discuss every conceivable problem that you will encounter in getting a new business started. Some problems occur so frequently, however, that they seem almost epidemic. To be forewarned is to be forearmed.

Personnel problems

Be careful whom you hire. Be sure to provide adequate supervision, furnish the necessary training, and create an environment in which people will be self-motivated.

Precautions

- Never hire anyone unless you both know exactly what that person is to do.
- Be aware of the cost of training new employees, and budget for it accordingly.
- Recognize that a new employee may not reach peak efficiency for several weeks or even months.

Executive control

Differences frequently arise between partners, co-founders, or key executives in a new business. The smaller the business, or the less experienced the individuals, the more likely you are to experience such problems.

Precautions

- Be sure, at the very outset, that everyone clearly understands and accepts the division of authority within the company. Everyone needs to know precisely what responsibilities belong to them and what responsibilities have been assigned to someone else. Adhere to that delegation of responsibility rigidly, or work out a change in that delegation together.
- Learn to work as a team. Most problems can be resolved more quickly and satisfactorily by taking the team approach.
- Above all, select people who want to be accountable and who have the record to prove it.

Many people abhor paperwork, but accurate, up-to-date records are absolutely essential to a successful business.

Precautions

- Determine what records are needed, who is to maintain them, the format that is the most useful, and the frequency with which they should be reviewed. Too much paperwork can be as wasteful as too little.
- Decide who is to be privy to the information in your files, in what format, with what frequency, and for what purpose.
- Determine how long each type of record should be retained, where, and by whom. Who is to dispose of old records, when, and how? Are there legal reasons for maintaining certain records (tax records, for example) for a specific period of time?

Poor sales

If you are experiencing a negative cash flow, it may be primarily due to inadequate sales.

Suggestions

- Don't wait for business to come through the door. Go out and look for it.

- Many entrepreneurs lack marketing expertise. Perhaps the company needs a sales manager.
- You may need a larger and/or more experienced sales force.
- You may have developed other segments of the company, such as production, far faster than your sales volume.
- Your cash-flow projections may be faulty. If you're inexperienced at that sort of thing, seek help.
- Review your product concept. Is your product or service out-dated, overpriced, or noncompetitive?

Poor inventory control

If you find yourself over-stocked with either raw materials or finished product, it's costing you money.

Precautions

- Analyse the turnaround on orders. If it's not necessary to fill orders from existing inventory, try to pace the production to the rate of incoming orders.
- Pay close attention to stock turnover, materials requirements, order rates, and purchasing and inventory schedules.
- Determine what has caused your imbalance and decide how to correct it. Is this a temporary solution or a permanent solution to the problem?

Lack of cash

There never seems to be enough money. Entire books have been written about this problem and how to deal with it.

Suggestions

- Look for new sources of capital. Increased sales would help, of course, but survival is the most important thing, even if it means giving up a percentage of the business. Just don't wait too long!
- Review your current sources of capital. Are you paying too much interest? Can you find other, less expensive financing?

- Do you have some asset that can be converted to cash? Could you, for example, sublet some unused portion of your building, store, or office?
- How much cash do your customers owe you? Ask them to pay up on time if they buy on credit and try to negotiate shorter credit terms for future sales.

Pricing

If you are satisfied with your sales volume but unhappy with your net profit, your pricing could be at fault.

Suggestions

- See how your prices compare with those of competitors. Are you underpriced? This might increase your sales volume, but it will hurt your profit margin.
- See if you can't get a better price for your product or service by enhancing its quality or quantity. Not everyone shops on the basis of price alone.
- Is there a way to reduce your cost of sales? Buying in larger lots? Reducing the size of your sales force? Adjusting your promotional budget?

PLAN FOR PROFIT

There is an axiom that applies to every successful business: if you put something in, be sure to get something out. That something, of course, is profit.

Profit doesn't just happen. You must plan for it. It is your primary business objective, and you must give it the time and attention it deserves.

If a company does not produce a profit, it is a hobby, not a business — an avocation, not a vocation. This suggests that you must treat your business like a business, not a hobby. Think like a business person and act like a business person. Be professional. Respect your customers, your prospects, your employees, and your competitors.

Strive for excellence, not only because it is the best way to attract and retain customers but because it is good business. Callbacks, returns, unpaid receivables, and claim for damages by dissatisfied customers cost money and eat into the profits. One of the best ways to maximize profit is to do the job right the first time.

When you become the head of a company, you must stop being task-orientated and learn to be leader-orientated. Not only does the success of the company depend on it; the livelihood of your employees depends on it too.

For many entrepreneurs, the hardest and perhaps the most distasteful part of running a company is the administrative (paperwork) part of the job. Successful entrepreneurs learn to overcome that and do what must be done. If you are not directing the company, you are really acting like nothing more than a super-employee — a supervisor or a foreman. Others can be hired to handle the company's work, but only *you* can make the critical business decisions. You are the boss.

You may delegate certain responsibilities to other people — bookkeeping, sales, advertising — but you are the one who must provide the guidance for these people. In the long run, they are merely doing a job. You are leading the company.

Here are some of the things you must consider in your new role.

Banking

It is important to establish a separate bank account for the business and not to mix company funds and personal funds. The law required it of partnerships and corporations, and although not required by law, it is a wise step for proprietorships to take, too.

Proprietorships must complete a tax return each year, so having a bank account will help to make the preparation of this form easier. But even more important, the maintenance of a separate accounting system and bank account will help you manage the company more efficiently. If you need to borrow money, decide to take in a partner, or wish to sell the business at some future time, a good set of financial records will make it much easier for you to establish the company's actual worth.

The failure of a partnership or a corporation to keep company money and personal money separate might cause the Inland

Revenue to argue that the business is not a separate taxable entity. In that case, the owners might be forced to include all of the company's income on their individual tax returns. Creditors might charge that the corporation is not properly organized and that the owners should therefore be held personally liable for the company's debts.

Don't take chances. Keep the family finances and business finances totally separate. Some people even keep their personal and business accounts in separate banks to avoid confusion or possible error.

Bookkeeping

Have you ever written a cheque and forgotten to enter it in your cheque-book? Then you have some idea of the trouble a business can be in if a receipt is lost or mislaid, if a sale is not recorded, or if a similar error in bookkeeping occurs.

Maintaining up-to-date books and records will help you prepare your tax returns and other business reports in a more accurate, more timely, and less costly manner. Again, doing the job right the first time proves to be a valuable business axiom.

Profit is measured according to some simple rules. Taxable profit is not the same as the cash you have or the cash you are owed. Profit is usually the difference between the sales you have invoiced and the cost to you of producing and selling the goods or services which make up the sales figure. The costs which are set against the sales figure are what you paid for any goods resold plus the costs which have been incurred during the period in question (the financial year for example).

What the above means is that you may be spending money on things which are not part of the calculation of this year's profit. For example, if you buy 100 units and sell 50 of them, only the cost of the 50 you've sold can be set against the income. The rest are counted as stock or inventory at the price you paid for them or their market price if that is lower than cost price.

If you buy a car or a machine, only the cost of using that car or machine for the period in question is counted. The calculations of what it does 'cost' is usually based on some accepted formula. For example, if the car costs £12,000 and is expected to last for six years, then the 'depreciation' — the cost of the use of the car — is £2,000 per year. Other methods of calculating the amount of depreciation tend to put a greater loss in the earlier years. For tax purposes, the Inland Revenue has a method of calculating the amount of depreciation you can charge in a year, called the Capital Allowance. The amount you estimate to give a realistic picture of profit or loss may not be accepted for the calculation of tax.

A principle adopted by the accountancy profession and accepted (in principle) by the Inland Revenue, is that future gains are never anticipated but future losses are. Of course, the losses must relate to the period in question. Income is counted from the time you send out the invoice, not when you get paid!

If some of the customers don't pay their bills, a gain (your profit) will have been incorrectly anticipated. To compensate for this possibility, some of the profit is set aside in a reserve. This reduces the amount of taxable profit. Any bad debts which you know about are either written off from this reserve or directly from the profit. At the end of each period the reserve is readjusted according to the situation.

Although bad debt provision is properly conservative, don't let it give you the feeling of security. A £1,000 invoice which is not paid costs you £10,000 worth of sales if your net profit margin is 10 per cent. Make sure you chase your customers for payment and if you don't trust them, make them pay cash. If they will not pay cash, do not supply them, let someone else end up with the bad debt instead.

Setting the financial year

Although the determination of your company's financial year may seem like a minor issue, it can be of considerable significance to a newly formed company. By selecting the most favourable tax year, it may be possible, for example, to defer income or expenses to a more advantageous tax period.

Such a decision could also provide a number of tax advantages for a firm's founders or owners. The company could begin business in April, for instance, but elect to have its financial year end on the following 31 January. The company could then defer payment of compensation to the founders/owners until January, thereby deferring their income taxes on that compensation until the following year.

Proprietorships and partnerships are limited to using the financial year which ends on April 5th. Companies can select their own financial year.

The payroll

Handling the payroll involves more than writing and distributing cheques for the employees. Withholding taxes and National Insurance payments are also involved, and, if they are not handled properly, you may be personally liable, even if the company is incorporated. If that should occur, those penalties cannot be discharged through bankruptcy.

Short of that, simple lateness in making payments to the government can subject you to rather stiff penalties.

Engaging an in-house accountant or even an outside firm to handle these chores for you does not absolve you of the ultimate responsibility. Therefore, be aware of these matters and keep a watchful eye on the manner in which they are performed.

Insurance

An uninsured loss could wipe you out. Being under-insured could have the same effect. Protect yourself, your business, your family, and your employees by being sure you have an adequate amount of insurance coverage.

These insurances are mandatory:

Employers liability
Motor insurance

Below are some of other insurances available which are recommended. You may also have signed a contract (e.g., when hiring equipment) which requires you to provide insurance.

Fire and other perils
Loss of profits
Theft
Loss of money
Goods in transit
Credit insurance
Public liability
Product liability

Professional indemnity
Legal expenses
Key person insurance.

The last can be particularly important to a new business. If one of the key people in the organization were to die, there might be no way to fill his or her position, and the company could die as well. If the partnership agreement (or shareholder's agreement) specified that a deceased partner's interest (or shareholder's shares) must be liquidated, the survivors may not be in a financial position to do so — unless there is insurance.

When the business is a proprietorship, the death of the owner endangers not only the assets of the company but the proprietor's personal assets as well. Without insurance, the death of such an individual could leave the survivors bankrupt.

There are many other legal, accounting, and record-keeping considerations to be weighed. A seasoned accountant and/or solicitor can be of far greater value to your business than the fee you will be asked to pay for the service. The decisions that are made at the beginning will stay with you for quite some time, so they must be made wisely and with future growth in mind.

10
Market your business

DEVELOPING A MARKETING PLAN

It is faulty reasoning to assume that you will draw business simply by hanging up your sign, opening the door, and waiting for the customers to file in. Successful marketing depends on the development and execution of a viable marketing strategy, or plan.

First of all, it is important to understand what is meant by marketing. Marketing is the means by which you convert your resources (human, material, and financial) into products or services that fulfil a need in the market-place as the consumer perceives such a need.

Take another look at those last seven words. If you devise a better mousetrap, but the consumers do not perceive the need for a better mousetrap, you are not likely to be successful. On the other hand, if the consumers perceive a need for, say, a CB radio, a home computer, or a VCR — whether or not any such need truly exists — then companies offering those products are likely to enjoy a substantial amount of success. The *need* does not have to be genuine, but the *perception* of a need does.

Of course, needs may be stimulated, even manufactured, by a clever business. The use of advertising, for example, often helps to create the perception of a need when, in fact, no such need exists. Although this may be an effective tactic for the short term, it is not a good business strategy for the long term, and entrepreneurs should base their business on a product or service for which a genuine need actually does exist.

How, then, does one develop a sound marketing plan for a new business?

You will want to consider seven critical factors.

1 What circumstances are critical to your success?
2 What business strategy should you use?
3 What do you know about the market?
4 What do you know about the competition?
5 What sales tactics should you use?
6 What pricing policy should you adopt?
7 How should you promote your business?

Each of these key questions should be explored in depth. The more thoroughly you investigate, analyse, and resolve these questions, the greater your chances of success.

Circumstances critical to success

- Fully define the business you are to be in.
- Who and where are your customers?
- What profit margin is realistic? (Consult Dun & Bradstreet and ICC Information Group Ltd, both of which keep track of the average net profit for business in a variety of fields.)
- How much sales volume do you need to break even? To show a profit?
- Can you employ sufficient help? Will your help be experienced and capable, or will you have to provide training?
- Can you buy materials at a favourable price? From a reliable source?
- Are you flexible enough to make some changes if changes become necessary?

Your business strategy

- What need does your product or service satisfy?
- How is your product or service different from that of the competitions?

- Will you sell direct to the consumer? To wholesalers, jobbers, agents, or sales reps? To some other company or group of companies? To an agency of the government? To some combination of these?
- How much stock or inventory should you maintain?
- Will you produce one product or service, or will you offer a variety?
- In what direction(s) do you expect your company to grow? Have you a plan for encouraging and directing that growth?
- Have you gathered data from all of the readily available sources? These include

  Public libraries, especially those with specialist business information sections (see appendix 5)
  The Department of Trade and Industry's regional offices (appendix 2)
  Local Enterprise Agencies (see BIC in appendix 1)
  Local Authority Planning and Industrial Development departments
  Trade Associations
  Trade Press (See *British Rate and Data* in your local library)
  Colleges, polytechnics, and universities

- Have you considered engaging professional help in analysing the marketing data that you have accumulated? It is easy to arrive at a conclusion that would appear to be correct statistically but that actually may be false.

  Example: If one simply divides the size of the total market (say, £10 million a year in sales) by the sales volume (say, £1 million a year) that the company hopes to attain, one could conclude that the company would have to capture a 10 per cent share of the market in order to reach its sales objective.
  Often, however, 20 per cent of the market will produce 80 per cent of the demand for a particular product or service. Therefore, only 20 per cent of the total customer base is buying £8 million worth of the product or service each year, while the remaining 80 per

cent makes just £2 million in purchases each year.

If your company were successful in reaching the critical 20 per cent of the customers who do most of the purchasing, it would need a market share of only 2.5 per cent to reach an annual sales volume of £1 million. A company that cannot penetrate this elite group and that must garner its sales solely from the larger but less influential portion of the market would have to attain a 40 per cent share of the market in order to reach the £1 million sales level.

- How big is your market today? How big will it be in five years? In ten years?
- What are the characteristics of the market? Is your product or service most appealing to a special age group, sex, ethnic culture, economic level, industry, or geographic sector? How often do your customers buy? How much do they buy? Are the sales seasonal or do they even out year round?
- What are the major trends in the industry? Are you ready for any foreseeable changes? Will your company be leading the way toward a change or merely following along?
- What are the major applications of your product or service? Can you envisage any others?
- Who will be your major customers? Do they differ from the profile of an 'average' customer? How? Should this affect your marketing efforts in any way?
- Are you meeting the requirements of the customers and of any regulatory agencies that may be involved?
- Should you add — or eliminate — any product or services?
- Have you talked to any of your prospective customers? What were their reactions?
- If you are manufacturing a product, how will it be distributed? At what cost? What are the acceptable delivery schedules?
- How are you providing for field service or product support? What is this likely to cost? Have you budgeted for the cost?
- Have you established a policy regarding warranties or

guarantees? Have you budgeted for the cost?
- Have you test marketed your product or service? Have you identified from the customer's point of view, its functional requirements? Its market appeal?
- Have you considered possible joint venture projects?
- Are you sure that you are not over-extended — trying to do more than you are capable of doing?
- Are you sure that your marketing goals are appropriate? Do they focus on such things as number of customers purchasing, size of orders, orders per customer, repeat orders, total unit volume, and market share?

Analysing the competition

- Who are your competitors? What are their strengths and weaknesses? How does their specific product or service compare with yours?
- Are there any potential competitors that you can identify?
- What market share does each competitor now hold? Where do you expect to get your share of the market?
- In what specific ways are your competitors vulnerable that can ease your entry into the market?
- If there is no apparent competition, are you sure you have a viable product or service? If you are breaking new ground, are you sure that some other company will not be able to capitalize on your efforts, move into another field, and take over your clientele?

SELECTING YOUR SALES TACTICS

- What potential customers will you be contacting? In what order? When? How?
- How large a sales force will you need? What volume should you expect from each salesperson?
- Have you established workable sales territories?

- How long will it take to provide a satisfactory level of sales volume?
- Will you have any limitations on orders (a minimum order quantity, perhaps)? How will you pursue repeat orders?
- Will the sales force be salaried or commissioned? Will you offer bonuses or incentives?
- Have you dissected the market into meaningful business segments? Identified the size and growth potential of each segment? Identified the potential customers in each segment? Established marketing objectives and strategies for each segment?

SETTING A PRICING POLICY

There are a number of ways to establish your pricing policy. Take the advice of an accountant and select the one that is best for you.

Skimming

This technique is often useful to the entrepreneur who is bringing out a truly new product or service. Since there is virtually no competition, the company places a high price on its product and aims at a very select audience — those who are willing to pay the extra price for something new, unique, different, out of the ordinary, or best. The product becomes a prestige item, and the company's profits are high, thereby providing the capital for growth, expansion, and new product development or product enhancement.

Later price reductions open up new markets, until eventually the product matures, the profit margin levels off near the industry norm, and the market nears saturation.

Some examples of this sort of strategy include the CB radio, the personal computer, the Trivial Pursuit board game, and the compact disc player.

There is a drawback to this strategy: because of the high prices and profits, competitors are encouraged to produce market imitations of the product. Some of them offer their product at a lower price, pushing prices down.

Those who select this pricing strategy must be prepared to change prices quickly in order to meet the new competition. They must be extremely careful, after the encouragement of their early success and the resulting high profits, not to over-extend or over-produce themselves.

Cost-plus pricing

One of the most common pricing strategies in business is the cost-plus method. Essentially, this means that the company calculates the cost of their product and then adds on a set percentage of that figure to establish an acceptable level of profit.

Obviously, this is a handy strategy for retailers. If a company buys its product from a manufacturer for, say, £10 per unit; then decides it wishes a gross profit of, say, 30 per cent; and then determines that its overhead (rent, advertising, utilities, wages, etc.) amounts to, say, 50 per cent of its total sales volume, then it simply prices the product at £19.50.

$$\text{(cost of product + gross profit) + overhead = sale price}$$
$$(£10 + £3) + £6.50 = £19.50$$

Some companies, especially new ones, may choose to base their calculations on projected costs rather than historic ones.

The cost-plus process is similar for other types of business, although the formula may vary according to the way the firm keeps its records. A company might prefer, for example, to express its profit margin as a percentage of its total cost rather than as a markup on purchases:

$$\text{(cost of product + overhead) + gross profit = sale price}$$
$$(£10 + £6.50) + £4.95 = £21.50$$

The amount of profit is higher using this formula because the company is taking a markup on its overhead as well as on the cost of its product.

Note

Whatever variation of this strategy one may select, the selling price *must* cover the total cost of the product plus a percentage for profit. Failing to cover all one's operating expenses will result in under-pricing, a loss of profits, and possible financial ruin.

Low pricing Many new businesses tend to under-price, rather than over-price. The philosophy seems to be that you can draw more business if you under-sell your competition. There are a number of basic flaws in this philosophy.

You may be able to sell for less than your competition if you can buy for less, if you have less selling cost, or if you can make up for the reduced margin of profit by selling a far greater volume than the competition.

On the other hand, you must realize that the competition could respond by cutting its own prices, possibly triggering a price war. A price war, particularly one of any duration, can be disastrous to a struggling new company.

One should consider, too, that a company that expects to work on an exceptionally small profit margin (typical of those who employ this pricing strategy) will require a far greater amount of capitalization at the outset to help it weather the lean, cash-hungry start-up period.

Loss-leader pricing Companies that offer a wide range of products or services often attempt to attract new business by offering some popular item at a price that is at — or even below — their cost. The concept is to cover that loss with profits from the sale of other merchandise that the customer is expected to buy while on the premises. Groceries, chemists, and department stores often employ this tactic, but it is seldom used by smaller or speciality types of business.

Opportunity pricing When there is a serious shortage of some product, a company may seize the opportunity to raise its price on the product, realizing that some customers want or need the product enough to pay the higher price. This is a short-term situation, of course, and once the shortage no longer exists, prices must — and will — return to normal. Those who adopt this pricing policy run the risk of alienating some of their customers who resent being apparently overcharged during the period of the shortage.

Manufacturers may select one of these pricing strategies, or in response to varying conditions in the market, they may opt for one of the following, all of which are more applicable to a mature firm than to one that is just getting started. These strategies are included here for two reasons: Firstly some entrepreneurs are going to acquire established businesses, rather than start new ones, and secondly the companies that are being formed today will become mature firms in just a few short years.

Protective pricing A company may have an exciting new product, but it may also have a large stock of other products that it cannot afford to dump. In such circumstances the company may set a high price on the new product until its stock of older products has been depleted, then lower the price of the new item in order to broaden its market.

Similarly, the manufacturer of a low-cost product may make every effort to keep the cost low, thereby discouraging competitors from entering the market.

Or a manufacturer may retain a high price on its product until a competitor appears and then begin to lower its prices. If the manufacturer plans to withdraw from the market, it may decide to retain the higher price and allow its market share to diminish gradually until its stock is finally depleted.

Adversity pricing Actually just another form of protective pricing, this policy is designed to help a company stay in business until more favourable market conditions exist. Basically, it means pricing the product at a level that will cover out-of-pocket costs (and possibly some of the overhead), thereby enabling the company to keep operating and retain its key personnel while waiting for business conditions to improve.

Obviously, this is a short-term policy that ought to be employed only under severe circumstances, such as a major recession. It will draw heavily on the company's cash reserves.

When considering your pricing alternatives, be sure to ask yourself these questions:

- What are your competitors' pricing policies? Should you imitate them or use another policy? Why?
- Is your pricing policy likely to change over a period of time? Why? When? How?
- Are you planning to offer a volume discount? Have you established a rational policy for it?

- Perhaps most important of all, does your product or service fall within an acceptable price range to be competitive in the marketplace?

MARKUP VS. MARGIN

Terminology can create many problems. An example is the use of the terms *markup* and *margin*.

Markup is a percentage of the *cost* price whereas *margin* is normally a percentage of the selling price.

For example, you purchase a product for £10 and sell it for £12.50. The £2.50 is a 25 per cent *markup* as calculated thus:

$$\frac{\text{Increase in price}}{\text{Cost price}} \times 100 \text{ per cent, or:}$$

$$\frac{2.5}{10.0} \times 100 = 25$$

The £2.50 is a *20 per cent* margin on selling price calculated thus:

$$\frac{\text{Increase in price}}{\text{Selling price}} \times 100 \text{ per cent, or:}$$

$$\frac{2.5}{12.5} \times 100 = 20$$

Knowing the *margin* required, you can work out the selling price from the cost price as follows:

$$\text{Sale price} \qquad \frac{\text{Cost}}{\text{Cost as a proportion of sale price}}$$

Example You purchase the product for £10 and want to sell it for a 20 per cent margin, making the sale price of the article £12.50

$$12.50 = \frac{£10.00}{\cdot 80^*}$$

For the sake of experience and for a thorough understanding of how to use this formula to calculate the profitable sale price for a product, see if you can work out the following problems:

1 You purchase a dress from the manufacturer for £18.95 and you want a margin of 35 per cent when you sell it. How much should you charge for the dress?

2 You paid £15 for a radio and sold it for £18. What margin did you realize?

3 You believe that you can sell a great many pocket calculators for £12.95, but you want to realize a margin of 15 per cent on each sale. At what price must you be able to buy the calculators?

4 You have purchased some blankets for £29.95 and want to price them so that you will realize a margin of 30 per cent. What selling price will you place on each blanket?

5 You bought a large shipment of refrigerators for £200 per unit. Your markup is 25 per cent. What price will you charge for each refrigerator?

Answers

1 £29.15
  100% — 35% = 65% (or .65)
  £18.95 ÷ 0.65 = £29.15

2 16⅔%
  £15 ÷ £18 = 83⅓%
  100% — 83⅓% = 16⅔%

3 £11.00
  100% — 15% = 85% (or .85)
  £12.95 × 0.85 = £11.00

4 £42.79
  100% — 30% = 70% (or .70)
  £29.95 ÷ 0.70 = £42.79

5 £250.00
  £200.00 + (25% x £200.00) =
  £200.00 + £50.00 = £250.00

If you had any difficulty in solving these problems, think of some typical situation that you are likely to encounter in your

*As your margin is 20 per cent of selling price, your cost is 80 per cent

business and solve those problems using this formula. Keep practising until you are really adept at calculating the cost of an item, the percentage of markup, and the selling price. This is a skill on which you will have to rely quite often.

Discount, an often-confusing term (sometimes called markdown), is a percentage that reflects a reduction in your selling price. It is calculated as follows:

$$\text{Discount or markdown} = \frac{\text{Amount of price reduction}}{\text{Original selling price}}$$

Example: You have reduced the selling price on an item from £12.50 to £11.25 (an amount of £1.25), resulting in a markdown of 10 per cent.

$$10\% = \frac{£1.25}{£12.50} \times 100$$

Again, it is well worth the time to gain experience in working with these formulas. See if you can answer the following problems:

1 You have a TV for sale at £595. A customer offers you £550 for it. What discount would this represent?
2 You have decided to offer a 50 per cent discount on all of your £14.95 items. What will the new price be?
3 You have reduced your line of £79 coats to £59.95. This represents how much of a discount?
4 You have marked down a stereo set by 25 per cent and are now asking £300 for it. What was your original sales price?
5 Your accountant suggests a 20 per cent discount on all of your £37.50 sportswear. What will the new sales price be?

Answers

1 7½%
   £595 — £550 = £45
   £45 ÷ £595 = 7½%
2 £7.48
   £14.95 × 50% = 7.48
3 24.11%
   £79.00 — £59.95 = £19.05
   £19.05 ÷ £79 = 24.11%

  4 £400
     If 75% (100% — 25%) = £300, then 100% (the original
     price) = 100 ÷ 75 × 300 = 400
  5 £30.00
     £37.50 x 20% = £7.50
     £37.50 — £7.50 = £30.00

Once more, if you had any trouble solving these problems, think
up some situations of your own, solve them, and learn to
become familiar with the process of computing discounts.

PROMOTING YOUR BUSINESS

A budget for the promotion of the company and its products
should be considered part of your cost of doing business. Have
you included promotion in your budget? How did you arrive at
the figure that you set? Is your budget consistent with the industry average? (New companies often budget more than established
companies because they obviously are not as well known in the
market-place.)

What medium or media will do the most effective job of reaching your customers and potential customers?

 • TV
 • Radio
 • Newspapers
 • Consumer magazines
 • Trade magazines
 • Direct mail
 • Billboards
 • Point-of-sale displays
 • Trade shows

Have you apportioned your promotional budget so that it provides specific amounts to be spent on each of those media that
will do the best job of reaching your market?

If you lack promotional expertise, have you selected advertising and/or public relations advice to help you? Have you provided for their fees in your budget?

Are you prepared to promote consistently? Hit-and-miss promotional efforts are not as effective. Too many businesses have the faulty impression that the only time to promote is when sales are down. A consistent, well-targeted promotional campaign is by far the most effective.

Have you really analysed what message you wish to use in promoting customers and prospects?

Have you fully explored the image that you want your promotional campaign to create for the company?

Assuming some of your promotion (advertising) will be designed to produce enquiries about your product or service, have you established a suitable follow-up procedure?

If you are using advertising to generate sales by mail, have you established a routine for receiving and filling the orders?

Do you have brochures that illustrate and describe your product or service? Operating manuals? Service manuals?

If you are doing business through agents, wholesalers, or jobbers, have you prepared a suitable catalogue for them? Have you provided them with the necessary sales literature, product specifications, and the like?

Getting down to basics, have you:

- Announced the formation of your new company, telling the public what business you are in, where you are located, and your business hours?
- Announced who the officers and other key people in your company are?
- Set up a procedure for announcing any new products or services that the company may offer?
- Designated someone within the company to assume the responsibility for its ongoing promotional programme?

Richard Hearn
Winter Inn

Richard Hearn always had a taste for an interesting, good value holiday. His career had taken him from being an overseas rep. on self-drive camping holidays to General Manager of a subsidiary of a major holiday company. Then, in early 1984, disaster struck — the parent company closed down the subsidiary. Richard managed to buy one of their trading names — Winter Inn — and with that, a lot of contacts and £5,000 in cash he started to put together his own holiday business.

The trick, as far as Richard was concerned, was to aim carefully designed holidays at a very well defined set of target customers. Most successful small businesses know their customers and sell them just what they want to buy.

Using the trade name Winter Inn, Richard and his wife Linda contacted good quality French and Belgian hotels and designed short-break car and cross-Channel ferry weekend holidays. Now all they had to do was reach the customer.

Winter Inn's target customers were well-off professional couples who read the 'quality' daily newspapers. A half page advertisement in the *Guardian*, for example, was far too expensive for them and in any case a simple advertisement lacked real credibility as far as the reader was concerned. So, instead of using the advertising space, Richard offered the travel writers a free weekend holiday.

The resulting write-ups brought a huge response. One Saturday article in the *Guardian* produced 800 phone calls over the weekend and 2,000 enquiries altogether. Nearly 4,000 enquiries came from writeups in just three quality newspapers.

Winter Inn went from strength to strength. Inn Ski was added providing cross-country skiing holidays. Then came Summer Mountain Holidays; unusual, attractive and special and a change of the general operating name to 'Inntravel' to cope with their year-round operation.

From their small beginnings in 1984 Richard and Linda have a business turning over about £½m in 1987 and are now going for the million.

11
Business finances

DEVELOPING A FINANCIAL PLAN

Along with a marketing plan, every business should have a carefully thought-out financial plan to reflect the company's current economic position and to provide guidelines for future growth and expansion.

Although you may not have had any formal training in finance or accounting, you should — as quickly and as thoroughly as possible — learn some of the terminology, learn how to read a profit-and-loss statement, and learn to ask questions of your financial advisers that will help you stay on top of your ever-changing financial situation.

Money is the name of the game: Money to buy materials, machinery, or products. Money to pay salaries. Money to finance research and development. Money for expansion. Money for profit after all the bills are paid. It is almost impossible to run a successful company without knowing not only where the money is coming from and where it is going but what is happening to it along the way.

A useful financial plan will cover your past history (a new company, of course, will not have any financial history), your present condition, and the company's likely financial needs for the future. All three are important.

Your past history will be helpful to you in the event you need to go outside the company for funds. Nearly every lending source will want to know your track record before it decides how much money to lend you and on what terms. Your past financial record also is the best way to tell whether the company's performance is improving or declining, and in what areas.

Your present financial condition should be reflected by:

- An up-to-date profit-and-loss statement (P&L)
- Details of your credit arrangements and sources
- Revenue projections
- Ratios and comparative analyses (internal, external, and budgetary)
- Contingent liabilities
- Insurance
- Tax conditions
- Methods of review and control

Your future needs should be reflected by:

- An equity statement
- Your capital requirements (amount and purpose)
- Sources of funds (internal and external)
- A financing proposal

RATIO ANALYSIS

Perhaps the least familiar of these financial tools are the various ratios that have been formulated to determine the economic 'health' of a company.

Liquidity ratios measure the company's ability to repay short-term obligations as they come due.

Profitability ratios help determine how profitable the company is.

Turnover ratios measure how many times per year the company turns over its debtors, stocks or creditors. The term *activity ratios* is sometimes used.

Trading ratios show how well the company is utilizing its productive assets by measuring the number of dollars that are produced by a given level of working capital or total assets.

Leverage ratios measure how much creditors vs. owners have invested in the company.

To make use of these guides, you must gather the company's past and current financial records. You can then prepare a ratio trends chart that will show your company's position. You can compare the position against previous results, if you have them, and against the results you planned to happen. You can sometimes obtain the average results for your industry from trade associations, Dun & Bradstreet, Inter Company Comparisons Ltd or Jordans Ltd. (Banks may also have industry averages drawn from their own records, though they do not publish them.) Industry averages give some performance benchmarks, but the information is only as good as the data published by the companies. Consequently, they cannot be relied upon as the only comparator to your own figures.

Liquidity ratios

● To measure your ability to repay short-term debt

$$\text{Quick Ratio} = \frac{\text{Quick assets (Current assets} - \text{Stock)}}{\text{Current liabilities}}$$

● To indicate your cushion of current assets over current liabilities

$$\text{Current ratio} = \frac{\text{Current assets}}{\text{Current liabilities}}$$

Profitability ratios

● To evaluate the pretax return on your assets

$$\text{Return} = \frac{\text{Pretax profits}}{\text{Total assets}}$$

● To determine the pretax return on your net worth

$$\text{Return} = \frac{\text{Pretax profits}}{\text{Total assets} - \text{Total liabilities}}$$

● To assess your pretax profit on sales

$$\text{Profit} = \frac{\text{Pretax profit}}{\text{Net sales}}$$

- To measure your percentage of gross margin

$$\text{Gross margin percentage} = \frac{\text{Net sales} - \text{Cost of goods sold}}{\text{Net sales}} \times 100$$

- To determine your expense ratio

$$\text{Expense ratio} = \frac{\text{Total operating expense*}}{\text{Net sales}}$$

Turnover (activity) ratios

- To calculate turnover of accounts receivable

$$\text{Turnover} = \frac{\text{Net credit sales}}{\text{Average debtor balance}}$$

- To measure the time receivables are outstanding

$$\text{Days outstanding} = \frac{360}{\text{Debtor turnover}^\dagger}$$

- To determine inventory turnover

$$\text{Turnover} = \frac{\text{Cost of goods sold}}{\text{Average stock balance}}$$

- To calculate how long your stock stays in inventory

$$\text{Days in stock} = \frac{360}{\text{Stock turnover}^\ddagger}$$

- To measure turnover of creditors

$$\text{Turnover} = \frac{\text{Total purchases}}{\text{Average total creditors balance}}$$

- To see how long your creditors are outstanding

$$\text{Days outstanding} = \frac{360}{\text{Creditors turnover}^\S}$$

* Or any other expense item
† See previous formula.
‡ See previous formula.
§ See previous formula.

Trading ratios

- To evaluate the turnover of your net working capital

$$\text{Turnover} = \frac{\text{Net sales}}{\text{Average net working capital}}$$

- To assess the turnover of your total assets

$$\text{Turnover} = \frac{\text{Net sales}}{\text{Average total assets}}$$

Leverage ratios

- To determine your debt-to-net worth ratio

$$\text{Ratio} = \frac{\text{Total liabilities}}{\text{Net worth} - \text{Intangible assets}}$$

- To determine the ratio of cash earnings to current maturities of long-term debt

$$\text{Ratio} = \frac{\text{Net earnings and noncash charges*}}{\text{Current maturities of long-term debt}}$$

An analysis using these various ratios can be very helpful in identifying your areas of financial strength and/or weakness, helping you to make sounder financial decisions and gaining a better understanding of how bankers and other financial people evaluate your business. They can help you to plan for improvements in the company's financial performance and to plan a loan request, when needed.

Knowing your debt-to-net worth ratio, for example, can help you regulate your debt to best advantage. If the ratio is high, you are said to be highly geared. This is a disadvantage if the rate of interest you are paying is high. It is an advantage, on the other hand, if you are earning more from the assets than you are repaying in interest.

*Depreciation and amortization

By knowing how many days you have had goods in stock, one of the turnover ratios, you will be able to determine whether you have obsolete or slow-moving items.

Comparing the number of days your creditors are outstanding with the number of days your debtors are outstanding, two other turnover ratios, you will know the *credit gap* between your creditors and debtors.

Having too many pounds in sales supported by too few pounds of net working capital or total assets, a condition called *overtrading*, can lead you to trouble because one large slow-paying debtor could decimate your cash flow. Low ratios, on the other hand, may mean that you are unprofitably overinvested in net working capital or total assets. An analysis of your trading ratios can help keep you on track.

Analysing these business ratios should become a scheduled part of your routine. They can be most helpful if they are performed regularly. Evaluate your data not only against the industry averages but against your past performance and against your company's overall performance goals.

BREAK-EVEN ANALYSIS

For a brand-new business, a break-even analysis is particularly important. It will help you to set prices, control expenses, make better business decisions, and improve your business planning.

To calculate the sales break-even point for your business

1 Determine your *fixed costs* — those items that remain the same regardless of your sales volume. These might include rent, salaries, office or administrative costs, interests, and depreciation.

2 Determine your *variable costs* — those that you incur specifically to make (or buy) and sell your product. These might include materials, direct labour and manufacturing overhead, and sales commissions.

3 Some items seem to be neither fixed nor variable. Such *semi-variable costs* might include advertising because advertising costs increase in steps as your sales increase but not in exact proportion to sales. Determine what your semi-

variable costs are and allocate each item either to fixed or variable cost, whichever it seems most natural to fall under.

4 Total your fixed and variable costs.
5 Calculate your contribution margin (sales minus variable costs).

● To evaluate your contribution margin as a proportion of sales

$$\text{Proportion of sales} = \frac{\text{Contribution margin}^*}{\text{Total sales}}$$

● To determine your sales break-even in pounds

$$\text{Break-even in pounds} = \frac{\text{Total fixed costs}^\dagger}{\text{Contribution margin proportion}}$$

Example A bakery produces bread and cakes. The average sales per week is £1,000. The cost of the flour and other materials is £300 per week and the cost of sales commission is 5 per cent, (£50 per week). The remainder of the costs are 'fixed' and total £585. The contribution *margin* is £1,000 − £350 (£650). The contribution *proportion* is 0.65, (£650 ÷ £1,000). the break-even sales in pounds is £585 divided by 0.65 (£900).

● To determine your sales break-even in units

$$\text{Contribution margin} \div \text{total units} = \frac{\text{Contribution margin}}{\text{per unit}}$$

$$\text{Break-even in units} = \frac{\text{Total fixed costs}}{\text{Contribution margin per unit}}$$

Example The bakery sells 2,000lbs of produce a week of various styles. The contribution per lb is £0.325, which is calculated by dividing £650, the contribution, by 2,000, the output in units, (£650 ÷ 2,000 = 0.325). The break-even volume in terms of lbs is calculated thus: £585 (the fixed costs) divided by the contribution margin per lb (£0.325) giving a break-even quantity of 1,800lbs per week.

* See 5 above
† See previous formula

Use these formulas regularly as a means of:

- Estimating the sales volume necessary to reach your profit goal.
- Determining the effect of cutting your fixed or variable costs.

Although not directly essential to your break-even analysis, statistics will also be useful.

- Return on investment (net profit divided by the capital invested by the owners of the company). The larger the ROI, the more attractive the company will be to investors.
- Return on total assets (net profit divided by total assets). This figure represents how profitably you have used all the company's resources.

You may find these calculations difficult at first but they are crucial to good business management. Work through them slowly with a pencil and paper. If you cannot understand them, ask your business adviser to teach you, or go on a short training course until you can do them easily and understand the results.

READING A P&L

A company's Profit and Loss Statement (P&L) is the handiest indication of your success or failure. It's a basic business document and you should be able to read one as easily as you can read the football results.

The P&L indicates where your revenue is coming from and where it is going. By taking enough time to review the figures occasionally, you will be able to determine what areas are costing you too much money, what operations are not producing enough income, and so on. From this, you can fine-tune your business plan to put your financial picture into better balance.

Study the sample P&L in table 7.

- What does it tell you?
- What might this company do to reduce costs?
- What can you tell about the company's cash reserves?
- What can you learn about its cash flow?

● How can this information be useful to you?

Go over your P&L with your accountant for several months until you feel competent to read and analyse the document on your own.

Remember that the P&L is an *action* document. It will serve little purpose in a ledger of a file folder. It should be used as a tool to help you improve your business and your business planning.

Know your costs

One of the things a P&L can tell you is your costs. What they are. Where they come from. How they compare with the industry averages. How they relate to your income.

You have some control over your costs, of course, but you have a great deal more control over your pricing structure. A thorough knowledge of your costs will allow you to price your product or service profitably.

Cost containment is a never-ending process. The more your costs increase, the more you must charge for your product. If the price gets too high, you may no longer be competitive; indeed, the product itself may become obsolete if a newer, less expensive alternative comes onto the market. (Witness the way plastics have replaced metals in many products, and the way integrated circuits have taken over the field of electronics.)

By keeping a careful eye on critical cost areas, you may be able to take corrective action before a crisis occurs. If a supplier has consistently raised prices, for example, you may need to arrange a meeting to discuss alternatives, such as buying in larger quantities in order to earn a lower unit cost. You may even have to seek another, less expensive supplier.

An analysis of your costs also may reveal areas in which you are spending about 7 per cent of sales on promotion, for example, and your P&L shows that you have been spending only 4 per cent, you may wish to increase your promotional budget.

12
Manage yourself and your business

WHAT SUCCESSFUL BOSSES DO — AND DON'T DO

Leaders are made, not born. Genes do not dictate who will or will not become a great leader.

Somewhere along the path through life, however, successful leaders do acquire certain common characteristics:

- They develop confidence.
- They learn to put their time to good use.
- They become people-orientated and goal-orientated, not task-orientated.
- They acquire the team concept.
- They learn to delegate skilfully.
- They become flexible in their thinking. If one approach doesn't work, they seek out and employ another.
- They sustain their enthusiasm for their work.
- They learn the value of good preparation.
- They constantly strive to improve their personal skills.
- They look to the future rather than to the past.

While learning to do these things, and do them well, successful leaders also learn that there are a number of things to avoid:

- They are not authoritarian. Tact works better.
- They do not dwell on *who* caused a failure, but on *what* and *why*.
- They do not clutter their organizations with deadwood.

Instead, they replace non-performing individuals with competent, enthusiastic, well-motivated people — and keep them that way.

- They promote not on the basis of tenure but on the basis of performance.
- They do not shackle their people with a lot of unimportant rules, regulations, and conditions.
- They do not dominate the decision-making process. They welcome and encourage the input of others.
- They do not set unrealistic goals.
- They do not over-extend themselves or their companies.

Successful leaders abandon the routine tasks and concentrate their time and attention on just three things:

1 Planning the direction and growth of the organization
   (a) For today
   (b) For the future
2 Developing the organization itself by
   (a) Hiring good people
   (b) Training those people
   (c) Channelling the work flow properly
   (d) Retaining top performers
3 Motivating their employees

PMA OR PYS?

Your approach to the job has a great deal to do with your success or failure. Productive people approach their work with a positive mental attitude (PMA). Non-productive people frequently adhere to the philosophy of 'protect your ass' (PYA).

Obviously, the former is an enthusiastic, optimistic approach. The latter is a cautious, guarded, suspicious approach.

While the individual guided by PMA is achieving one goal and setting her sights on the next, the one who is concerned with PYA is double- and triple-checking every step she takes for fear of doing something wrong. One is an achiever; the other is a plodder. One welcomes a new challenge; the other fears it.

PMA stimulates innovation; PYA preserves the status quo. PMA encourages teamwork; PYA discourages it for fear the individual will be unjustly blamed for somebody else's foul-ups. PMA may give a person the tendency to be overzealous and even rash, but PYA causes people to be excessively cautious, even secretive, about what they are doing.

You will find yourself trying to hold rein on the individual with PMA. You will find yourself constantly calming and reassuring, prodding and cajoling the individual with PYA.

SOMEBODY HAS TO MAKE A DECISION

All of us have a measure of PYA in our natures. No one likes to make mistakes. As a result, we all have a natural inclination to avoid making decisions — particularly unpopular ones. Still, somebody has to do it.

Perhaps these suggestions will make the decision-making process easier:

- Define the problem. Be specific. Use quantitative terms such as time, pounds, or units. State your primary and your secondary objective(s).
- Gather all the available facts.
- Line up all your alternatives. Make no attempt to evaluate or prioritize them now; just list as many as you can.
- Consider the consequences of each option. Be specific, and try to use quantitative terms: how much time, money, and manpower will each alternative require? Are those resources available? List all the long-term consequences. If you use resources today, will you be leaving yourselves short for tomorrow's needs?
- Select the most viable alternative.
- Test your selection. Discuss it with key people. Discuss it with those who will be most directly affected. Try to draw out any obstacles or objections to the plan, and have a back-up plan ready.
- Announce your decision.
- Sell your decision. Present the facts as you see them. Point out the weaknesses in the other plans. Respond to any known objections, and explain how you will overcome

each of the known obstacles. By word and action, let it be known that you are committed to the decision you have made.

- Implement your plan. If possible, give the idea a limited test before you go full-scale with it. Be prepared to make modifications or corrections, if necessary.

Some problems, you will find, seem to defy solution, no matter how hard you try. The reason may be one of these:

- Subordinates often hesitate to criticize their superiors.
- People sometimes tell you what they think you want to hear rather than reveal their true feelings.
- Urgency often stimulates unreliable judgement.
- Personal conflicts may work against a constructive, cooperative solution.
- Those who feel responsible for having created or contributed to a problem often become self-protective.
- People sometimes lack the ability to see a situation from any viewpoint but their own.
- Distasteful situations tend to create tension, fear, and uncertainty.

You will have to be able to overcome these tendencies if you are to get to the bottom of the problem and formulate the right decisions.

Decision making needn't always fall on the shoulders of one individual. In fact, most decisions — and many of the best — are reached through collective effort. Gather your most knowledgeable people, present the problem, and see if they can come up with a solution. If they come up with two, both of equal merit, then you may have to serve as the tie breaker.

'Group think' does have a few potential hazards to watch for, however. Beware of these:

- Occasionally, everyone in the group will get along famously. There will be no disagreement, but no one will speak the truth or disrupt the harmony within the group.
- A group may use rationalizations instead of taking corrective action.
- Instead of seeking innovative ideas or quality decisions, a group may take the easy way out and fall back on loyalty, teamwork, or cohesiveness as a way to work the company through a problem.

● Polarization may occur between those for and those against
the decisions of the group. This is a very difficult to deal
with because you can be accused of playing favourites no
matter which side you take.

Above all, try to base your decision on facts. Do not make
assumptions. There is an old business proverb that says, 'Don't
ASSUME. It'll make an ASS out of U and Me.'

Use this test to determine your decision-making index (DMI).

Test your DMI
(Decision-Making Index)

	Never	Rarely	Occasionally	Often
1 Do you let the opinions of others influence your decisions?				
2 Do you procrastinate when it's time to make a decision?				
3 Do you let others make your decisions for you?				
4 Have you missed out on an opportunity because you couldn't make a decision?				
5 Do you tend to study so many details that it's hard to reach a decision?				
6 After reaching a decision, do you tend to have second thoughts?				
7 Did you hesitate while answering these questions?				

Score one point for each *often*, two for each *occasionally*, three
points for each *rarely*, and four points for each *never*.

If you scored 25-28, you are very decisive and probably have no problem assuming responsibility for the choices that you make.

If you scored 15-24, decision making is difficult for you. You need to work at being more decisive.

If you scored 14 or below, you're going to have big problems running a business unless you learn to overcome your timidity. When a decision has to be made, face up to it and do it!

MANAGING YOUR CASH FLOW

Business is based on the ebb and flow of money, and what you do with it as it passes through your hands.

We've defined net profit as the difference between income and expenses (minus taxes). But we haven't yet considered *cash flow* — the movement of funds in and out of the company. Cash flow can be the difference between success and failure in a new and growing company.

By way of illustration, let's say you have a small company with a monthly payroll of £5,000. You are eagerly seeking business, and you consider yourself fortunate to land a job that will pay £50,000 for one month's work. The job will tie up all your personnel for that month, and you will have to lay out £25,000 for materials with which to do the job. Still, the gross profit is attractive — £20,000 (£50,000 minus £25,000 for materials and £5,000 for salaries). It seems like a nice piece of work.

For the sake of illustration, however, we now are going to assume that your customer turns out to be something of a deadbeat. Oh, he's good for the cash, but he decides to take his sweet time to pay it. Meanwhile, you have had no other income for an entire month, you owe £25,000 to the people from whom you purchased the materials for the job, and you have to meet a £5,000 payroll. You are out of pocket £30,000 — and you haven't received any income for over a month.

What if the customer doesn't pay his bill for six months? What if your company were to come across six deadbeat customers in a row? All outgo and no income. Could your bank account stand it? What if any one of those customers proved to be a bad debt and *never* paid his bill?

That is the essence of cash flow: the ability to bring in enough money to pay the expenses and maintain a satisfactory cash reserve for the unexpected.

A high level of work is fine. A good method of cost-control is great. But you need that inflow of cash to keep your company going. Otherwise, your cash reserve is going to evaporate, and you may find yourself in the unenviable position of heading a company that is doing beautifully on paper, but that is dead broke as far as the cheque book is concerned.

Here are some pointers on ways to help assure an adequate cash flow:

- Know what your capital requirements are, for the month, and for the coming year. If you know what your expenses will be, you can plan your work so an adequate cash flow will be available.
- Establish a credit policy that is beneficial to you. When you extend credit to someone, that person is enjoying the use of your money. If it isn't necessary, don't offer credit to a customer at all. If extending credit is essential to your business, see if a local bank won't handle the lending arrangements so you will not have to tie up your own capital. If you absolutely must extend credit on your own, put limits on the time and the amount.
- Put the terms of your agreement in writing to avoid a variety of problems beyond description, prepare a simple document that shows what you will do, when, and on what terms; what your fee will be; what the customer is to do, when, and on what terms; the penalty if you fail to perform; the penalty if your customer fails to perform.

   Misunderstandings often result in slow or non-payment. Failure to get the money for the product you sell or the service you perform will disrupt your cash flow and erode your profitability.
- Use inducements for prompt payment, such as a discount for cash on delivery. Many companies dealing in services use this technique. Some even attempt to receive payment in advance by offering a discount for pre-payment. (There is a potential danger to this. You should consider such money as being held in trust for service not yet performed. If you spend it today, you may have to provide the service

out of pocket when the customer demands your service at a later date.)

● See if you can't get a partial payment up front and the rest in prescribed increments. Contractors often use this type of financial arrangement, obtaining one-third at the beginning of the job, one-third at a specified midpoint in the job, and the final third when the job is completed.

● Watch your buying habits as carefully as you do your income. If you buy from a supplier who is going to charge you monthly interest or carrying charges, you must include those charges in your cost of doing business, or it will eat into your profits. For example you are in the electrical business and have purchased £1,000 worth of lighting fixtures for a job you are doing. Your supplier applies a 1 per cent carrying charge to your outstanding balance each month. The job takes several weeks to complete, and your bookkeeper takes another week or so to prepare the invoice. The customer takes another thirty days to send you a cheque. The post eats up several more days, but on receipt of the cheque, you pay your supplier.

Two months or so may have elapsed since you ordered the lighting fixtures and went on your supplier's books. With two months' carrying charges, those fixtures now cost you £1,020.10, not £1,000. If you charged your customer £1,000 for the fixtures 'at cost', you have lost £20.10 on the transaction. That £20.10 will come from your profits.

● Stock costs money. Try to buy what you need when you need it. Even if you purchase your stock with cash, thereby eliminating any finance charges that might be charged by a supplier, you are tying up capital that otherwise could be used to produce income. Let's examine another example.

You are in the appliance business, and you maintain an average stock of £50,000 worth of refrigerators, which you pay for on delivery. Your bank is paying 5¼ per cent on the money you have in your current account. A year-end sales analysis shows that you turn your entire stock of refrigerators once every six months, and you receive a markup of 10 per cent on each sale.

In other words, you have done £100,000 worth of business in refrigerators over the year, having turned your stock twice. You have earned a gross profit of £10,000 on those sales (10 per cent). On the other hand, you have tied up £50,000 in capital that, were it in your current account, would have earned you £2,625 in interest. Therefore, you have actually realized less than three-quarters as much profit on your investment as you might have thought (£7,375 rather than £10,000, due to the loss of interest on your capital).

Had you invested only, say, £25,000 in stock, and turned that stock every three months instead of every six, your actual gross profit for the year would have been £8,687.50 instead of £7,375. And if it were possible to do business with a stock outlay of only £10,000, you could increase your profit figure to £9,737.50.

Stock does cost money. We realize that suppliers often provide attractive discounts when you purchase in volume and/or pay for their shipments in cash. We also realize, however, that many retailers pass those savings on to their customers by lowering their sales prices, so the principle remains the same. Keep your stocks as low as possible, consistent with the needs and expectations of your customers. When possible, let your suppliers do your warehousing for you.

● Whether it be stock or some other form of expense, be careful not to over-extend. If you do not know where the money will come from, don't spend it — no matter how attractive the offer may be.

● Don't let stubbornness destroy your liquidity. If a customer refuses to pay, it may be better to negotiate than to fight, even if it means losing all the profit on the job. Tact is nearly always superior to temper, as shown by the following example.

You have done a £20,000 job for a customer who now, for whatever reason, says he's dissatisfied and will not pay his bill. There was £2,500 worth of profit in the job. You have determined that it would be expensive to take the customer to court. In addition, it would be time-consuming and there even might be the possibility that the customer files for bankruptcy before the matter can be settled.

By maintaining a calm and businesslike posture, you may

be able to gain payment by reducing the customer's bill by £1,000. He might jump at the bargain and you would at least recover your expenses plus £1,500 in profit.

The longer the issue remains unresolved, and the longer your money is being tied up, the less likely it is that there will be a satisfactory resolution of the situation, and the greater the risk of losing your entire investment.

We are not suggesting that you forsake any of your legal rights or that you pursue every practical means of obtaining payment. But the key word is *practical*. Justice is not always swift or, for that matter, just — and there's generally a price to be paid in terms of solicitor's fees, court costs, time lost from work, damage to one's own reputation, the loss of future business, and so on.

- See that your statements go out promptly. The objective is to receive payment as soon as possible after the sale is made or the service is rendered.

  An unpaid bill is an IOU — and you can't deposit an IOU in the bank. If you have £30,000 in debtors on your books, it is the same as having made £30,000 worth of interest-free loans to your customers.

It is the assurance of a satisfactory cash flow that allows a company to pay its bills on time. This can be particularly important to a new business. Cash flow not only avoids the costly assessment of interest on overdue bills, but it establishes the company as a responsible organization with which to do business, produces a solid credit rating, and relieves management from the concerns of indebtedness that divert its attention from more important matters, such as future growth and prosperity.

MANAGING YOUR TIME

People often talk about 'finding time' or 'making time' to do something. Both are foolish expressions, of course, because you cannot find or make time; all you can do is make a determined effort to manage your time so that it will be put to best use.

Some people are more proficient at this than others. It is not surprising to discover that they consistently outproduce the others.

When you are wasting time or not getting the most that you can from it, it's usually due to one of the following causes: lack of organization, interruptions, procrastination, daydreaming/ lack of concentration, and motivation.

Lack of organization

Two plumbers of my acquaintance have totally different work habits. Both work an eight-to-six day, but one is barely making ends meet while the other is prospering nicely. The difference stems from their work habits.

Plumber 1 records every incoming customer call in sequential order. Every morning, he assigns each of his people to a job; when one of the employees completes a job, he or she telephones the office and gets a new assignment. The dispatcher always assigns the worker to the next unanswered call on the waiting list.

Plumber 2 spends the final half-hour of each day organizing the following morning's calls in geographic order. In the morning, instead of going to the shop, one employee will go northwest, one will go southwest, one will go northeast, and one will go southeast. If there are no calls to be made in the southeast but a lot of calls in the northwest, two people will go to the northwest. Usually, a worker can go from one job to another in the same end of town for at least half a day and never stop to call the office until the prescheduled work assignments have run out. When that happens, the dispatcher gives the employee one or more additional assignments, usually in the same end of town.

Plumber 1 has employees running all over the city, wasting time on telephone calls to the office and wasting even more time travelling from pillar to post. Plumber 2 keeps his people working as much of the day as possible, making fewer phone calls and doing far less travelling between jobs.

Plumber 1 averages about four jobs per man-day, while Plumber 2 averages nearly twice that number.

Plumber 1 gets about half the productivity (and revenue) per employee that Plumber 2 does. Furthermore, Plumber 1 spends roughly four times as much on the petrol, oil, van maintenance, and equipment replacement as Plumber 2.

Better organization is the key to one company's prosperity versus the other's.

You can benefit from this example. Spend a few minutes today to organize your work for tomorrow. The time you spend will be well rewarded.

Begin with a list of the things you need (want) to accomplish tomorrow. Determine which of those tasks can be delegated to someone else. Arrange the remaining items in one of the following ways:

- By *priority*
  Example: Most important things first; least important last.
- By *the clock*
  Example: Mrs. Jones's appointment at 8:00, followed by Mr. Smith's appointment at 8:30.
- *Geographically*
  Example: Proceed from 105 High Street to 21 Sheep Street to 31 London Road.
- *Sequentially*
  Example: Attach trailer to truck, drive to Oxford, load parts on trailer, and then drive back.
- By *reasonable likelihood of success*
  Example: If you have a 90 per cent chance of selling a job to Mr. Brown, a 10 per cent chance with Ms. Black, a 30 per cent chance with Mrs. White, and a 70 per cent chance with Mr. Green, schedule a call on Brown first, Green second, White third, and Black fourth.

  Example: If Mr. Brown's, Ms. Black's, Mrs. White's, and Mr. Green's companies all have shown an interest in buying your product or service, but Mr. Brown's company is likely to spend £5,000 a month, Black's company £7,200 a month, White's company £3,000 a month, and Green's company £1,200 a month, call first on Black, second on Brown, third on White, and fourth on Green.

Interruptions

Interruptions take up time and break your concentration. To avoid interruptions, consider doing the following:

- Engage a secretary to screen all calls and intercept all visitors.
- Ask a subordinate to answer your least important callers and talk to your least important visitors.
- Don't attend every conceivable meeting. Let subordinates represent you and report on the highlights.
- Ask for written, rather than verbal, reports.
- Adopt a modified open-door policy. Let the employees know that they should expect to talk to you at certain times of the day or days of the week.
- Let sales reps (or customers, for that matter) know that you do not wish to be disturbed except by appointment.
- Eliminate all social calls from friends, members of the family, and so on.
- Conduct your business and then stop. Don't let letters, phone calls, personal visits, or business meeting ramble on.
- Develop your communications skills so that you do not have to repeat or explain what you already have said.
- Develop your listening skills so that you do not have to have someone repeat or explain what they already have said.
- Delegate decision-making authority to reliable subordinates so that workers can go to them with their questions rather than to you.
- Encourage subordinates to use their individual initiative in most cases, rather than ask your approval for everything they do.
- If an employee has a personal problem to discuss, do it before work, over lunch, or after work rather than during office hours.
- Get your secretary to schedule your business meetings for you so that you don't get involved in lengthy, nonproductive conversations.
- Cover all your business in one meeting or conversation rather than having a separate one for each individual topic. For example, one of your employees is responsible for the Smith account, the Jones account, and the Blackwood account. Ask that employee to update you on all three at one time instead of taking the time to get an individual briefing on each account separately.
- Learn to say no politely. When a subordinate says 'May I

see you for a minute?' say 'I'm pretty busy right now. Can it wait until our meeting tomorrow?' or, when a supplier says, 'Can I drop by to show you my new line?' say, 'Why not send me some literature on it, and we can get together if I'm interested.'

Procrastination

Procrastination is more prevalent among employees than among employers, but everyone has certain tasks that they dislike and prefer to avoid.

First, see if you can't delegate those unpleasant tasks to a subordinate. But if there are obligations that you simply can't avoid, try using one of these tips to help you overcome the tendency to procrastinate.

- Do the pesty job first. You're at your freshest then, and the knowledge that you have the distasteful job done and no longer have to think about it will give you an uplift for the remaining day's work.
- Set aside a particular time in your day, week, or month to handle the nettlesome project — and don't let anything get in the way. Putting off something can cause last-minute crises, slipshod work, errors, missed deadlines, lost business opportunities, and disgruntled business associates, employees, and customers.
- If the bothersome job is a time-consuming one, break it up into smaller segments. Doing a little bit each day will eventually get the job done — and perhaps with less aggravation.

Daydreaming/Lack of concentration

These are real time-wasters, and remember, it's your time!

Frequently, the cause of daydreaming or lack of concentration is similar to the cause of procrastination — a dull, uninteresting piece of work to be done. Once again, see if you can't delegate such chores to subordinates.

Other things that also could be causing the problem, however, are personal problems, fatigue, preoccupation with some other project(s), poor working conditions, such as noise or bad light, and improper diet, lack of exercise, or even a health condition.

As the boss, your behaviour sets the tone for your employees. You cannot afford to set a poor example. Therefore, if you daydream or can't concentrate, it is up to you to find a solution to it.

If you are suffering from poor diet, lack of exercise, or a health condition, see a doctor and strive to correct the situation. If you're bothered by poor lighting or noise, find yourself a more suitable office. If you are fatigued, make a determined effort to get more rest.

Preoccupation with other projects or personal problems can be the most difficult to offset, but you must condition yourself to take matters one by one, dealing with each in its own time and letting all others wait their turn. Sometimes you can relieve the pressure by delegating some of the work to others. Sometimes the only cure is to realize that you have taken on too much and would be better off foregoing some of the less important matters that are troubling you.

Poor motivation

Like procrastination, poor motivation is generally more of a problem among employees than it is among entrepreneurs. Employees have less freedom of choice about what they do, how they do it, when they do it, where they do it, and so on. An individual who has sufficient motivation to get a business going is much less likely to run out of steam as time goes by.

Of course, it can happen. Entrepreneurs tend to be a restless lot, and the daily routine of running a company often falls far short of the excitement that is part of starting one. I have known several individuals who have been extremely successful at starting new businesses and getting them well established, and then they sold them to others. To them, the thrill of starting a new venture is what they seek. They are perfectly content to let others assume the responsibility for its subsequent operation, growth, and development.

When an entrepreneur's enthusiasm begins to wane, it is a signal that some serious soul-searching needs to be done. Is there something else you would rather be doing? If so, perhaps you should sell the business or turn over the operation of the business to a partner or a subordinate and move on to something else.

It takes a highly motivated individual to start a business. Just as surely, a poorly motivated individual can destroy one. A wise person will get out of the business before allowing that to happen.

MANAGING CORRESPONDENCE

The timely handling of correspondence is important to any business — and is critical to some.

Establish a business-like policy towards the handling of correspondence, and be sure your employees know, understand, and follow the procedures that you establish.

Some rules of thumb:

- Designate one individual to receive and sort the incoming post.
- Be sure to expedite financial post — payments from customers, invoices from suppliers, orders. The day's receipts should be processed in time to be included in the same day's bank deposit. Prompt payment of suppliers' invoices often earns the company a discount, while late payment may result in added interest of carrying charges. The faster the orders are received, filled, and invoiced, the faster you will receive payment.
- Don't waste time on junk mail. Throw away that which is obviously worthless. Save the rest for review when you have some free time — while commuting, during leisure hours at home, over the weekend.
- Don't let correspondence accumulate. If possible, answer a letter the same day you receive it. If additional information is needed before an answer can be sent, ask for the necessary information at once and answer the letter as soon as you receive it.
- Don't allow subordinates' post to accumulate. Sales staff,

for example, may be out of the office for extended periods of time. Be sure there is someone to open, review, and respond to their post even if it is only to send the correspondent a brief note saying 'Ms. Young is out of the office until the twelfth, but you will be hearing from her then.' Urgent matters should be referred to a superior and/or relayed to the individual in the field by telephone.

● Read your correspondence carefully. If you're not sure what the correspondent wants, you can't send a sensible reply. There is nothing more frustrating than having to send someone a second letter when one should have done the job. The correspondent loses confidence in your capability, and the duplication of correspondence wastes your time as well as theirs. If your response involves enclosures, be sure they're included.

● Be sure important correspondence stays in the office. Many people make a habit of taking correspondence home or on a trip. Ask them to take a copy, not the original. Lost or mislaid documents can cause no end of trouble.

● Keep a carbon copy or photocopy of your outgoing correspondence. Does anyone else in the firm need to have a copy? Should anyone else in the correspondent's firm have a copy?

● Establish a workable filing system for correspondence. When you need to refer to a letter, can you find it quickly? Is all the correspondence related to a given project filed in one place? Have you provided for a prompt, efficient means of follow-up, if one is required? Have you established a procedure to screen and purge your correspondence files periodically? Have you properly identified documents that must be retained for legal or tax purposes and specified how they should be handled?

● Be sure you use the proper postage on your outgoing mail. Too little postage may result in delay, non-delivery, refusal by the recipient, and embarrassment. Too much postage is wasteful. (Note: There are a number of very profitable overnight delivery services in operation today. On occasion, these services *may* be necessary, but do not become addicted to them. Prompt response by mail — or even a telephone call when deadlines are tight — is a great deal less expensive.)

- Know the post schedule. It serves no purpose to answer a letter on the day it's received and then let it sit on a secretary's desk over the weekend. Try to get each day's correspondence into that same day's mail.

MANAGING FILES AND RECORDS

Few businesses, it seems, take the time or give the necessary attention to the proper maintenance of their files and records. As a result, they suffer either from not having enough documentation when they need it or from having rows upon rows of filing cabinets loaded with obsolete, incomplete, or otherwise useless material.

On the premise that 'you never can tell when you'll need a piece of string,' my grandmother saved balls and balls of twine that she'd salvaged from parcels sent to her over a span of forty years. I've known others who have similar collections of ribbons, bows, buttons, rubber bands, hardware items, and even shoeboxes. Grandma was not a good business person.

Bad record-keeping is one of the major causes of business failure among small companies. Good records, particularly sales and expense records, must be kept daily.

The law requires that certain documents be retained for various reasons, and it even specifies the length of time that one should keep them. Good business sense dictates that one also should keep the documentation related to any ongoing project. In addition, virtually every business will need to gather and retain a file of relevant and useful data, such as engineering, drawings, information on competitors, market research, personnel records, and so on. Careful attention should be given to what material is to be retained, in what manner, and by whom. These questions will be determined by the nature of the business, of course.

So much for having enough documentation. The other side of the problem is to decide what *not* to retain. It may sound like good philosophy to err on the side of keeping too much, rather than too little, but one always should be conscious of three things:

1 In a good filing system, you can locate what you need when

you need it. It is extremely difficult to try to find a needle in a haystack.

2 If the files contain outdated, incomplete material, there always is the possibility that it may be extracted and used, thereby causing embarrassment, producing errors, or — at the very least — creating confusion and wasting time.

3 It is costly to maintain files that have no useful purpose. The last figure I recall estimated the annual cost of maintaining files at something more that £3 per lineal foot. Since the average four-drawer filing cabinet takes up nearly seven linear feet of storage space, that equates to an annual cost of £20 per filing cabinet.

There are a number of ways to reduce excess filing and eliminate non-productive record-keeping.

- Avoid duplicate files. Frequently, a single letter may find its way into as many as half a dozen different files. Encourage everyone in the office to use a central file rather than separate files of their own.
- Avoid filing meaningless attachments. I have known people who file away *all* incoming correspondence, including junk mail and the envelopes that the mail comes in. Keep only what you need and will use.
- Condense your material. If you have read an article or a report that contains useful information, extract the part that is useful (noting the date and the source) and dispose of the rest. I have known people who file entire magazines rather than tear out the relevant page.
- Purge your files regularly. Typically, a piece of paper will go into the file and stay there indefinitely. Set up a procedure whereby all the files are reviewed and purged at least once a year.

13
Communication within your business

COMMUNICATING EFFECTIVELY

Effective communication involves both the ability to convey a complete message to the proper audience in a clear, concise manner and the ability to read or hear the message that is being communicated in such a way as to understand its meaning and avoid any misinterpretation of the meaning. Therefore, a good communicator must learn to express thoughts clearly, accurately, completely, and concisely; to listen attentively; and to ask pertinent questions when necessary. For example:

Poor: 'We must notify Johnson's that we are raising our prices.'

Better: 'Jo Kirkel (*delegating responsibility*) will notify Johnson's on July 6 (*setting a date*) that our prices are being raised by 10 per cent (*specifying the amount*) to offset the increasing cost of copper (*stating the reason*).'

When we speak of *internal communication*, we are referring to the messages that we convey to people within the company. Those that are intended for people outside the company are called *external communications*.

Internal communication includes a conversation, a memo, a telephone call, a letter, a company newsletter, a notice on the bulletin board, or any other means of conveying a message to the employees.

External communication employs most of the same media, but the audience may be a customer, a prospective customer, a supplier, a government agency, the citizens of the community in which we do business, members of the employees' families, or anyone else not on the payroll.

Since companies achieve their business objectives through the efforts of their employees, it is important for you to keep them informed. Otherwise, it is not reasonable to expect your employees to do their jobs well, on time, and in the most cost-effective manner. Examples:

- On June 1, the owner of a small manufacturing company in Glasgow decided to increase the price of his product by 10 per cent, effective July 1. He failed to convey this decision to his salesmen. On June 30, one of his salesmen closed a one-year £100,000 order with the firm's largest customer. Had the salesman known about the owner's decision, he could have delayed the deal *by one day* and earned the company an additional £10,000 on the contract.

- The proprietor of a large appliance firm in Bristol heard at a business luncheon that one of his customers, a home-builder, was in serious financial difficulty. He neglected to pass that information on to the salesman who handled the builder's account. The following week, the builder ordered and received appliances — ranges, refrigerators, microwave ovens, dishwashers, and disposers — with which to equip 100 new homes that he was finishing. Three week's after that, the builder went into bankruptcy — and the appliance company eventually received 30 pence in the pound for all the merchandise that the builder had purchased.

- A successful restaurant in Manchester owed its popularity to an extremely talented chef. The owner recognized this and was considering giving the chef a partnership in the business. The owner considered that the chef more than deserved it. But somehow the owner never got around to making the move or to telling the chef of his intention. Meanwhile, the chef began to experience a rash of personal and financial problems. Eventually, the chef was offered a higher-paying position with a restaurant in a neighbouring town — and he took it. The restaurant owner lost his chef, and then his clientele. Although the restaurant remains in business to this day, it has never gained its former popularity — because the owner failed to communicate with his employee.

The failure to communicate with those outside the company can produce equally devastating results. Examples:

- A number of years ago, General Motors decided that its Chevrolet *Nova* would be an excellent product to offer for the Mexican market. Thousands of cars were produced, but sales were disappointing. Finally, someone discovered the reason: *Nova* means 'won't go' (*no va*) in Spanish. A colossal bilingual communications booboo.
- The managing director of a small- to medium-size company had set a luncheon date with the purchasing agent of a very large corporation to discuss the terms of a very large contract. They were to meet at the Windhaven Hotel, but the M.D. by mistake went to the Brookhaven Hotel. While the purchasing agent waited at the Windhaven and the president waited at the Brookhaven, both parties became increasingly incensed, each feeling that he had been stood up by the other. It was several months before the facts of the situation became known. The company did not get its contract, and strained relations existed between the two individuals for a number of years.

An effective business organization thrives on cooperation and understanding. Good communication involves the flow of ideas, information, feelings, and perception.

Face-to-face conversations are better than telephone conversations. Written communications are better than oral communications. *Any* communication should be honest, direct, and complete.

What does one communicate to employees?

- *Good news* Recognition of individual or group accomplishment, favourable business barometers, noteworthy orders, new developments in product or service, the attainment of a goal, announcements of new and improved employee benefits, and similar achievements.
- *Bad news* It's better that they should hear it from you: the passage of unfavourable legislation, missed production objectives, increases in cost, slippage in sales or profits, lost

customers, missed opportunities, poor quality control, or other disappointing conditions.

- *Plans* What is proposed for the future, both short-term and long-term. What this means to the company and to the employees.
- *Policies* Guides to action, rules of conduct, strategies for the growth and development of the business, and basic commitments to certain relationships, actions, and responsibilities.
- *Changes* The modification of assignments, schedules, priorities, dates, standards, and procedures.
- *Rumours* Don't avoid them; respond to them with a forthright presentation of the facts.
- *What is expected* Let others know what they are supposed to do and not supposed to do. Set standards for quantity, quality, service, and cost.
- *How the company is doing* This is of particular interest when a company is new. Giving employees this kind of information gives them a way to gauge their performance and that of the company as well as a way to evaluate their contribution to the organization's progress.
- *Ways to improve* If the employees know what areas need improvement or how to accomplish it, they can be most helpful in bringing about the desired result.
- *Directions* Employees need to know *how* management wants things to be done.
- *Answers* Don't ignore employee's questions, suggestions, and complaints.

Your external communications should include the following:

- Additions, deletions, or changes in your product line.
- Price changes
- Changes in your delivery schedules or other business policies.
- Major new (or renewed) contracts.
- Important changes in your personnel.
- A decision to relocate; to add factories, stores, or offices; or to close a factory, store, or office.
- News about the company's financial performance.
- News involving employment, particularly if it will involve large-scale hirings or layoffs.

- Announcements regarding participation in trade shows or other local, national, or industry events of importance.
- Clarification of rumours, particularly any that may have an adverse effect on your business.

BE SURE TO LISTEN

One age-old philosophical question concerns whether a tree, falling in a remote and deserted forest, makes any noise. One faction argues that it does, based on the fact that whenever anyone is around to see or hear the falling of a tree, it most certainly does make a noise; ergo, all falling trees will make a noise. Another faction argues that it will not make a noise, because in order for there to be noise, there must be an ear to hear it.

The point is, communication does not exist unless the message is received and understood by the proper party. You can make phone calls, leave messages, put notes on the bulletin board, erect billboards, send a letter, a telegram, a memo, or even a smoke signal — but you are not communicating unless your message is being received and understood by the proper individual(s).

Communication is give and take; none of us is simply a 'transmitter' or a 'receiver'. We communicate because we have the ability to do both.

Unfortunately, not enough emphasis is placed on the importance of being a good receiver. We do not read carefully, and we do not listen attentively. As a result, we make mistakes, we leave jobs half done, we fail to do what we should, we do things that we should not, we get embroiled in unnecessary disputes — and so on and so on. A great deal of this could be eliminated if each of us were to learn to be a better listener.

It is estimated that the average person retains only half of a ten-minute presentation — and only a quarter two days later.

Being a good listener can be particularly beneficial to the entrepreneur because it:

- Encourages people to talk freely and frankly.
- Prompts people to discuss the things that are important to them.

- Stirs people to give you as much information as they can.
- Causes people to gain greater insight into and a better understanding of their problems, simply by talking them out.
- Helps people to see the causes of their problems and thereby helps them to figure out solutions to those problems.

There are a number of things you can do and a number of things that you should avoid, if you want to become a better listener.

Do:

- Be silent when it is someone else's turn to talk.
- Show that you are interested in what is being said.
- Let it be known that you understand — and are sympathetic to — the situation.
- Notice the body language that accompanies the verbal language.
- Listen 'between the lines' and determine what the other party is really trying to say.
- Ask questions.
- Try to determine what the other party may have that may have caused a problem or may be preventing the individual from finding a solution to a problem.
- Help the other party single out the problem and then see if they can isolate the cause of the problem.

Don't

- Interrupt.
- Allow other interruptions.
- Try to frame an answer before the other individual has finished talking.
- Pass judgement too quickly or in advance.
- Jump to conclusions.
- Give advice when it's not requested.
- Let yourself be swayed by the other party's opinions or sentiments.
- Let your attention wander.

Good listening habits will improve the quality of any decisions that you will have to make. Decision making involves the following sequence:

1 Get all the facts
2 Get all the opinions
3 Weigh all the facts and evaluate the opinions
4 Formulate your decision
5 Weigh the decision against the facts
6 Weigh the decision against the opinions
7 Modify your decision, if necessary
8 Announce your decision

ASK THE RIGHT QUESTIONS

There are various types of questions, and there are various questioning techniques. If a wrong question is asked, or if a question is asked of the wrong person, you are not going to get the answer that you want or need.

Types of questions

Factual
  1 Purpose
     (a)   To get information
     (b)   To open discussion
  2 Examples
     (a)   Who?
     (b)   What?
     (c)   When?
     (d)   Where?
     (e)   Why?
     (f)   How?
Explanatory
  1 Purpose
     (a)   To get reasons and explanations
     (b)   To broaden discussion
     (c)   To develop additional information
  2 Examples
     (a)   In what way would this solve the problem?
     (b)   What other aspects of the situation should we consider?
     (c)   How would this be done?

Justifying
1 Purpose
   (a)   To challenge old ideas
   (b)   To develop new ideas
   (c)   To get reasoning and proof
2 Examples
   (a)   Why do you think so?
   (b)   How do you know?
   (c)   What facts do you have?

Leading
1 Purpose
   (a)   To introduce a new idea
   (b)   To offer a suggestion of your own or others
2 Examples
   (a)   Should we consider this as a possible solution?
   (b)   Would this be a viable alternative?

Hypothetical
1 Purpose
   (a)   To develop new ideas
   (b)   To suggest another, possibly unpopular, opinion
   (c)   To change the course of discussion
2 Examples
   (a)   If we did it this way, what would happen?
   (b)   Another company does this. Would it work here?

Alternative
1 Purpose
   (a)   To decide between alternatives
   (b)   To get agreement
2 Examples
   (a)   Which of these solutions is best?
   (b)   Do you prefer Plan A or Plan B?

Co-ordinating
1 Purpose
   (a)   To develop consensus
   (b)   To get agreement
   (c)   To take action
2 Examples
   (a)   Can we conclude that this is the best way to go?
   (b)   Is there general agreement, then, that this is the
         plan we will follow?

Questioning techniques

Direct to group
1 Purpose
   (a)   To open discussion
   (b)   To change the course of discussion
2 Examples
   (a)   Where will we begin?
   (b)   What should we discuss next?
   (c)   What other factors are important?

Direct to an individual
1 Purpose
   (a)   To get special information or viewpoint
   (b)   To involve someone who hasn't been participating
2 Examples
   (a)   Sue, have you had any experience with this?
   (b)   Roger, what suggestions do you have?

Relay (referral to another person or group)
1 Purpose
   (a)   Allows the leader to avoid giving an opinion
   (b)   Gets others involved in the discussion
   (c)   To call on someone who knows the answer
2 Examples
   (a)   Would someone like to comment on Kelly's suggestion?
   (b)   Sally, how would you answer Bill's question?
   (c)   Marge, will you tell us what you have found out?

Reversal (referral to the person who asked the question)
1 Purpose
   (a)   Allows the leader to avoid giving an opinion
   (b)   To encourage the questioner to think individually and independently
   (c)   To bring out opinions
2 Examples
   (a)   How about giving us your opinion, Andrea?
   (b)   Kent, will you tell us what your experience has been?

HANDLING RUMOURS

One of the inevitable consequences of poor communication is

the rumour. When people do not know, they will speculate. And speculation breeds rumours.

Of course, rumours may arise no matter how well one communicates. That is why it is useful to know how to deal with such situations.

An advertisement by United Technologies Corporation addressed the matter head on. It read:

The snake that poisons everybody

It
topples
governments,
wrecks
marriages,
ruins
careers,
busts
reputations,
causes
heartaches,
nightmares,
indigestion,
spawns suspicion,
generates
grief,
dispatches
innocent
people
to cry in their
pillows.
Even its name
hisses.
It's called
gossip.
Office gossip.
Shop gossip.
Party gossip.
It makes
headlines

and headaches.
Before
you repeat
a story,
ask yourself:
Is it true?
Is it fair?
Is it necessary?
If not,
shut up.

(Reprinted with permission of United Technologies.)

When you find yourself beset by a rumour, the best approach is to reveal the facts as fully and as accurately as possible. If certain details are proprietary and sensitive to the welfare of your business, say so and explain the need for continuing to keep them secret. Otherwise, reveal whatever information is necessary to dispel the rumour.

Rumours, you will discover, often are self-inflicted. Realize that people — especially your employees — have a natural curiosity and an equally natural inclination to talk about their work. Give them accurate information to talk about.

Avoid keeping secrets or creating a secretive manner. If it is necessary for something to be kept secret, be sure that those in the know do not take advantage of the situation by gloating over those who are not. Decide if it's important to keep something secret; then decide if it's possible to keep it secret. Very often, the only way to maintain true secrecy is to keep things to yourself.

AVOID SURPRISES — EVEN GOOD ONES

Success may involve a degree of luck, but not as much as many people believe.

Entrepreneurs who wish to succeed will concentrate on developing a solid plan and then follow it step by step, toward their goal. They will encourage their personnel to do the same thing — which requires the highest degree of teamwork and co-operation.

Anything that interferes with a company's game plan will open the door to a variety of problems. Hence, surprises — either good or bad — are to be carefully avoided. Example:

A manufacturing company analysed its sales for the year and realized that it would have to produce at near-capacity levels to satisfy the needs of its customers. On the other hand, expansion would require a substantial amount of borrowed capital, and favourable interest rates were not to be found. Around midyear, one of the company's salesmen landed a large and totally unexpected order. Because of that, the firm was forced to rush into expansion, not only accepting the high interest rate that the bank imposed but paying a premium to the contractor for hurrying the completion of a new plant. While the new plant was being built shipments to the new customer had to be worked in with shipments to all of the company's previous customers, causing a number of late- or partial-shipment problems. Had the new contract been for just one year, the company would possibly have refused it — painful as that decision would have been. Fortunately, the contract was a multiyear agreement, which provided a great deal more security for the manufacturer who had been rushed into expansion.

A reverse scenario is easy to imagine. Our manufacturer might have opted to go ahead with the expansion in spite of the adverse interest rates on borrowed capital. Instead of gaining a significant new contract, he might have lost one. The consequences, quite obviously, would have been totally different.

A TV retailer projected the sales volume it might expect during the month of August, based upon past years' sales. She then concluded that her store could increase its share of the market during August by conducting a sale in which they would offer their product at a 30 per cent discount. To her surprise, a major competitor went out of business and offered its total inventory on sale at 40 per cent discounts during the month of August. Instead of selling *more* units during August, the retailer sold *less* — and all at a reduced profit. Fortunately, the retailer's sales *increased* during subsequent months due to the competitor's closure and the TVs she'd expected to sell at a *discount* in August eventually sold for *full mark-up* later on.

Surprises under the Christmas tree can be great fun. Surprises in business can cause a great many headaches for management. The right decision may be provident; the wrong one, disastrous. The best situation: take every possible contingency into account as you do your planning, allow some margin for error — and avoid 'surprises' as much as possible.

Roger McKechnie
Phileas Fogg fine foods from around the world

As Roger McKechnie frequently points out, Phileas Fogg are not snack foods, they are 'adult nibbles', the kind of thing that sophisticated party givers and social munchers need to match the other special things they have in life. But, in 1982, what was to become of a well-known brand of upmarket snackfood was just a dream for four ambitious partners working in a small wooden hut in the middle of a closed down steelworks. By August 1982, the dream had become a reality when the first products came off the production line of a small factory. A year later they sold £90,000 worth in one month alone.

The partners formed a great team. Roger was the managing director and he and the commercial director, Keith Gill, and the production director, John Pike, had come from one of the snack food industry giants. The marketing director, Ray McGhee, came from the advertising industry where he had worked on snack food accounts. Between them they had invested everything they had in the Phileas Fogg concept. It had to work.

Unlike their giant competitors, they could not afford to promote their product on television. They had to rely on their outstanding packaging design to attract the customers. They also had to persuade the supermarkets to put the product on the shelves and this was difficult to do because supermarket buyers want all their food products advertised on television. So, Phileas Fogg first appeared in small retailers, off-licences, pubs and other places where the target customers might go. The going was really tough at this stage, all the cash was tied up and the brand had to prove itself. Eventually, the sales record and the quality of production convinced some of the bigger retailers. As the company grew, it was able to start regional TV advertising in London and the South East where most of their customers were.

The growth record is quite phenomenal. The sales went from £1m in 1983/4 to £2½m in 1984/5, to £5m in 1985/6 and is estimated at £14m for 1988. The firm employs about 200 people. 'Without the strength of the team, all the people who work for us, and the commitment of our venture capital investors and bank,' says Roger 'the business would have not survived its own success.'

CONDUCTING MEETINGS

As the head of a company, you will be expected, if not required, to schedule and conduct a number of business meetings. Committee meetings. Planning meetings. Board meetings. Shareholder meetings. For some, this may be a brand-new experience.

A business meeting is not a social event. It is an opportunity to engage in some constructive 'group think', in which people with a common purpose exchange their individual knowledge to solve a problem or formulate a plan of action.

Your business meetings will be more effective if you:

- Schedule meetings only when they are needed.
- Always prepare and follow a strict agenda. Put the most important items first so there will be ample time to discuss them.
- Invite only those who need to be involved and who have something to contribute.
- Select a suitable meeting time and place.
- Discourage any and all interruptions.
- Stick to business and avoid digressions.
- Begin and end meetings on time.
- Be prepared before you enter the meeting.
- Steer the meeting toward its purpose — to reach some sort of decision or agreement.
- At the end of the meeting, summarize the conclusions and repeat the delegation of various responsibilities.
- Keep minutes and issue a follow-up report as soon after the meeting as possible.
- Follow up after the meeting to see that the matters discussed there are being resolved.
- After a committee has served its purpose, abolish it. Do not allow a proliferation of meaningless, time-consuming committees to exist.

One of the most frequent mistakes in business is to use a meeting as a means of communication. Meetings are not a good communication medium; written memoranda are far better.

14
Your employees

DEVELOPING YOUR EMPLOYEES

A company needs the kind of people who continue to learn as they gain experience, who acquire new skills and assume bigger responsibilities.

Normal turnover in a company always produces openings that must be filled. As the organization grows, new opportunities are created for those who have supervisory or management skills. When hiring new employees, it is wise to assess their potential for the future as well as their current capabilities.

It is not enough to hire people with potential, however. One of your top priorities should be to help the employees develop that potential.

Compare it to making improvements on your home. Adding a fresh coat of paint or upgrading the kitchen will make a house more valuable to you. In the same manner, helping your employees learn new skills and assume greater responsibilities will make those employees more valuable to you also.

You would not keep a large amount of cash in an old shoebox on some closet shelf. You would put it in a bank, where it draws interest and grows in value. Similarly, your personnel should not be pigeon-holed in dead-end jobs that inhibit their growth. Instead, they should be trained, challenged, and encouraged to do things that will help them — and the company — to grow.

Five years ago an American company instituted an in-house training programme that it calls its Entrepreneur University.

The electronic assembly company grew from $450,000 in sales in 1978, the year it was founded, to $3.6 million in sales in 1980, the year it began its management training programme. During those years, the company could not find enough experienced managers to oversee its rapidly growing number of personnel.

Over the past five years, this company's Entrepreneur University has trained 150 managers, from shop foremen to general managers. Meanwhile, its sales have grown to $80 million, and its total workforce has increased to 2,200 employees. Entrepreneur University costs the company about $500,000 a year, but management feels the benefits have far exceeded the cost.

Your employees are one of the company's most valuable resources — like money, real estate, and equipment. With the proper guidance, that resource can be made to 'appreciate' far more and far faster than any other.

THE MATTER OF COMPENSATION

Setting the amount of your own compensation as founder and head of the company is not a matter-of-fact consideration. It is one that should be given considerable thought — and should be discussed at length with your solicitor, accountant, and tax adviser.

Sole proprietors may set up virtually any arrangement that they wish. In a partnership, however, it is wise to have all the details regarding salary, bonuses, and other forms of compensation committed to writing.

When a company is incorporated and there is a single shareholder (as is often the case when an entrepreneur opens a new business), the owner should resist the temptation to treat the corporation's assets as his own. The tax consequences could be horrendous. Furthermore, it would probably be unwise for the owner to draw a salary that is any larger than he actually needs to live on because that only tends to drain the company's cash reserves and increase the amount of the owner's income tax. Since the owner can realize a long-term capital gain when he decides to sell his shares, a better approach would be to use the cash to expand the business and minimize the amount of his short-term taxes.

Key personnel within the company will also appreciate the advantages of a carefully planned compensation programme including, perhaps, short- and long-term incentives, tax-effective deferred compensation, and various types of fringe benefits.

In a new firm, cash is often scarce, and it is not feasible to pay large salaries. Good executives may still be drawn to the company, however, if they are offered a good long-term package.

Share schemes for employees are popular among young, growing companies. You need to take professional advice on the best way of introducing these schemes because the wrong scheme can have serious tax implications. Under certain circumstances the growth in value of a director's or employee's shares may be taxed as income, even when the shares are not sold. If you get the scheme right, the growth in value is taxed as a capital gain only when the shares are sold.

You can also give your employees options to purchase shares at previously agreed rates. This is a good incentive to employees to improve the performance, and hence the value of the business. For example, Dave joins the XYZ Company and is granted an option to purchase 10,000 XYZ shares for £1.50 per share (a fair market value at the time). Later, the shares rise to £3.00 and Dave elects to buy the shares for which he has an option. He pays £1.50 each for them. If he sold them for, say, £5.00 each, then he would pay capital gains tax on the £35,000 profit made from buying at £15,000 and selling at £50,000.

It is important to grant options under the Inland Revenue rules for approved share option schemes as there are further tax disadvantages if the schemes are not approved.

Another important area of benefit is retirement pensions. An increasing proportion of the population is becoming retired, so the demands on the state pension scheme are increasing, while at the same time there are less people working to contribute to it! The result will be a cutback in the benefits offered under the State Earnings Related Pension Scheme (SERPS). Currently employees and employers contribute to SERPS.

If you 'contract out' of SERPS into a private pension scheme, the government will refund that portion of your National Insurance contributions that would have been used to buy the SERPS benefits. In addition, as an incentive to change, they are offering to put an extra 2 per cent of each person's earnings between £2,132 and £15,860 into that individual's pension fund until 1993. Many companies will therefore have their own pension schemes in future, both for directors and other employees.

Private pension funds are available from banks, insurance companies, building societies and unit trusts. Company funds must be approved by the Inland Revenue. In many small companies, up to half the pension fund can be loaned back to the company to provide capital for buying assets such as premises.

MOTIVATION KEEPS MORALE HIGH

A recent hit song reflects the attitude of those who are not motivated by their work. The title of the song is *Take this job and shove it.*

The things that motivated previous generations — notably, steady wages — no longer provide the kind of stimulus that employees need. Today's better-educated, more highly skilled employees seek more from their work than just an income. A survey of 40,000 people conducted by the U.S. Chamber of Commerce revealed that employees value good wages behind job security in importance. Full appreciation of work done, feeling in on things, interesting work, good working conditions, promotion and growth within the company, tactful discipline, sympathetic help with personal problems, and loyalty to workers were also listed, in that order.

Employees are not motivated by management that:

- Ignores them.
- Takes them for granted.
- Does not recognize their preferences in matters.
- Belittles their accomplishments.
- Criticizes them in front of others.
- Is indecisive.
- Fails to perform its part of the job.
- Shows favouritism.

What does motivate a company's personnel is management that:

- Recognizes employees for work well done.

- Solicits ideas from the employees.
- Delegates responsibility.
- Identifies what is needed to do a good job.
- Acts quickly on employee complaints.
- Disciplines fairly and consistently.
- Sets a good example.
- Follows up.
- Prioritizes work assignments.
- Gets to know the employees.
- Builds a positive attitude.
- Presents job instructions clearly.
- Challenges them with important work.
- Provides the necessary support services.
- Lets them know what is expected.
- Keeps them informed of changes that affect them.
- Faces up to needed personnel changes and assignments.
- Demonstrates confidence in them.
- Encourages ingenuity.
- Promotes on the basis of merit rather than tenure.

BUILDING TEAMWORK

A successful business thrives on teamwork. Even when many functions must be performed independently, they eventually must come together in a smooth and efficient manner.

Consider the manufacture of a car. The body and frame may be made in one area, the bumpers and trim in another, the upholstery in still another. The headlights and the tyres may be produced by other manufacturers, in other locations. Yet all these components must come together in the right place, at the right time, in the right sequence: teamwork.

Imagine 20,000 cars sitting outside the plant without tyres on them!

Or consider food service. One individual may seat a customer, another may take the customer's order, and a third may cook the food. After the customer has finished, a fourth person may clear the table and prepare it for the next customer, while a fifth person is washing the dishes so that a new cycle can begin: teamwork.

What would happen if the chef failed to show up?

The existence — or lack — of teamwork is more visible in some lines of work than in others. The less noticeable it is, the greater the likelihood that it exists and is working nicely. Teamwork need not be obvious, but in any business establishment that involves more than a single employee, it is the only means of operating effectively.

Only a very small company can prosper through individual effort, and eventually it too will grow into an organization of people. Teamwork is what stimulates growth, minimizes waste, and increases profit. The lack of teamwork causes dissension, creates stress, stifles progress, causes accidents, induces waste, and foreshadows failure.

How does one blend a group of unique individuals into a team? Here are a few suggestions:

- Stress team goals.
- Focus on co-operation.
- While recognizing the efforts of individuals, do not stress the individual to the detriment of the team. This can create jealousies.
- Encourage competition between teams rather than individuals.
- Emphasize the importance of each person's job as it relates to the overall success of the team.
- Treat each individual as a valued member of the team.
- Show your people how to help each other.
- By word and action, show that you too are a part of the company team.
- Show your employees that the achievements of a team can be far greater than the combined achievements of its individual members.
- Select team leaders who are tactful and co-operative, not authoritarian or egocentric.
- Be quick to reassign those who threaten the success of the team. Such an individual might work out much better on some other team.
- Never show favouritism.
- Dispense praise to the team; express criticism only to an individual — and in private.

Teamwork is not a condition: it is an attitude, a frame of mind.

If you treat your employees like part of the team, they will perform like part of the team.

To have an organization, you must be organized. To be a leader, you must have something to lead.

In forming a company, what you're really doing is forming a team of people who will help you to accomplish your objectives.

DELEGATION OF WORK

The process of delegating work may sound more complex and mysterious than it really is.

If you ask a secretary to sort and open the day's mail, that's delegation.

If you assign different crews to different tasks, or ask somebody to go to the bank, or send a sales rep. to call on a client, that's delegation.

If an individual finds it hard to delegate work and responsibility, it's probably due to one of these factors.

- *Lack of patience* 'It's more time and trouble to explain what I want and how to do it than it is to do it myself.'
- *Insecurity* 'If I show someone else how to do it, they won't need me any more.'
- *Inflexibility* 'Someone else may do the job, but they won't do it the way I would do it.'
- *Inadequacy* 'If somebody else can do the job better than I, it will make me look bad in the eyes of others.'
- *Occupational hobby* 'I know it's not the best way to spend my time, but it's a job I like to do.'

Once they recognize these tendencies as flaws in their management technique, most people can overcome them with a little concentration and practice. After a while, delegation will come naturally and effortlessly.

Experience develops your skill not only to delegate, but also to delegate effectively. This involves what you delegate and to whom. Obviously, it is not very productive to delegate insignificant jobs to key people or to delegate critical jobs to incompetent people. Equally obviously, no employee can do an effective job if:

- There has not been sufficient time allowed to do the job.
- Sufficient resources (money, manpower, and materials) have not been allocated.
- Sufficient authority has not been delegated along with the work.

Along with the delegation of work comes the necessity to properly indoctrinate your employees with the basic concepts of delegation.

- They must appreciate the *need* for delegation. They must not feel that you are merely passing out favours to 'pets'. They must not feel that you are dumping off your own work on others. There is a difference between delegation and playing 'hot potato' or 'pass the buck'. They must appreciate the fact that assuming responsibility is a means by which they can grow professionally and can earn salary increases and promotions. They must see that delegation — at all levels throughout the organization — is a key ingredient of teamwork and co-operation.

- They must associate delegation with the attainment of certain goals and objectives. They must see the relevance of the work to which they are assigned. There must be general agreement on what is to be done, why, how well, when, in what priority, with what resources, and by whom.

- They must be taught the value of communicating with their superiors. Progress reports are necessary. If something is redelegated, a superior should know about it. If charges are made — in scheduling , for example — they must be communicated to a superior and to any other work unit that may be affected.

- They must be aware of your personal interest in what they are doing. Don't make them feel that you are looking over their shoulders. Don't stifle their initiative, imagination, and creativity. Don't encourage unhealthy rivalries between individuals or groups.

There are ground rules to follow that will make the process of delegation easier and more effective.

- Be careful in selecting the person to whom you delegate responsibility. Consider that person's interest in the work, training, experience, and personality.
- Remember that you retain the ultimate responsibility — and be sure that the employee realizes that, too.
- Be sure to create and stimulate a feeling of responsibility in the employee.
- Make the objective clear. Encourage the employee to ask questions.
- Delegate the 'what', not the 'how'.
- Be sure the employee understands the limitations of the assignment. Do not let them feel that they have *carte blanche* or are accountable only to themselves.
- Make sure you give the employee enough authority and support to do the job.
- Develop the employee's trust.
- Agree on the standards of performance that are expected.
- Establish checkpoints so that you — and the employees — can see what progress is being made.
- Assess the risks and provide for them.
- Give recognition when and to whom it is deserved.
- Take prompt corrective action when something goes wrong.
- Be willing to allow the employee a reasonable margin for error. Do not expect perfection. Be ready to accept a certain amount of failure.

EMPLOYEES NEED CAREER PATHS

More than ever, today's employees look to the future. They have seen their parents' jobs made obsolete by the rapid advance of technology, and they have no desire to be caught in a similar situation. They do not see their jobs as secure or plan to cling to them for the next twenty or thirty years. They see them as a stopover on their way to some other plateau.

This attitude is healthy for business. Ambition triggers hard work, ingenuity, innovation, and productivity. Complacency stifles them.

But because of this condition, today's employer is less able to place cut-and-dried labels on the organization chart. Work assignments — and the thinking of company management — must be more flexible. Job descriptions should not be too confining. Every position in the company must be open-ended — that is, the way in and the way out must be clearly indicated. People who begin to feel boxed in or in a dead-end will become dissatisfied and may leave, regardless of inducements such as salary increases, tenure, fringe benefits, and retirement plans. Today's employees want, need, and deserve a viable, visible career path.

Progressive management recognizes the value in this. As people gain new skills, they become more valuable to the company. As they assume greater responsibility, they free you to do other, more important things. As they attain their personal goals, they gain confidence, they strive harder, and they are happier. As they move up in the company, they push you up ahead of them.

Entrepreneurs who stifle the growth and upward mobility of their employees are stifling the growth of their businesses as well.

BECOME A COUNSELLOR

One of the best ways to determine whether your employees are satisfied with their work is to talk to them once in a while. They appreciate your interest — and you can find out a lot of things from which you otherwise may have been screened out.

Conferences with one or a group of employees are not the occasion to deliver either a sermon or a pep talk. They are an opportunity to encourage dialogue, an exchange of ideas, the frank and open expression of feelings. You can learn a great deal by listening. Give the employee(s) a chance to talk, and show that you are interested in what they have to say.

Let it be known that these are not complaining sessions. Those should be held at another time and handled in another way.

What should be covered during a counselling session?

- Let your employees know what's expected of them. Define their job duties and responsibilities, and discuss standards of performance. Stress teamwork and co-operation. Let them know what is required to earn a raise or a promotion.
- Let the employees know how they are doing. Appraise their performance against your standards. Identify their areas of real accomplishment, and designate the areas in which improvement is needed.
- Offer a plan for improvement, and orientate the plan to a single job weakness, rather than try to create a cure-all. Encourage the employee(s) to recommend other ways in which to improve. Agree on a plan together.
- Help the employee(s) implement the plan. Praise signs of improvement in their work, and encourage further effort. Correct their failures constructively. Teach by example, and review progress regularly with the employee(s).
- Reward the results that are achieved. Give praise, recognition, raises in salary, or bonuses. Increase their responsibilities, and promote them.

Selecting the time and place for counselling is important. Pick a time when:

- You are in a good mood.
- You believe the employee(s) to be in a good mood.
- Your relationship with the person(s) is at its friendliest.
- You are not rushed.

Never meet with an employee or employees immediately after he/they have suffered a glaring failure, not after he/they have a serious disagreement with you or some other superior.

Hold the meeting in a place where the atmosphere is not threatening or intimidating to the employee(s), and where everyone can be comfortable and relaxed.

A great many of the highly successful executives I have known will never hold an informal counselling session with an employee from behind a desk. The desk, even when it is not your own, represents authority and physically makes a barrier between you and the person with whom you are talking. What you are striving for is closeness, familiarity, and a relaxation of the tensions that often exist when an employee is talking to his boss.

APPRAISING AN EMPLOYEE

As an organization grows, it becomes increasingly difficult to know every employee, what she does, how well she does it, how to help her avoid mistakes, and how to help her improve. That is the reason for the appraisal interview.

In large organizations, department heads may handle this. In smaller ones, it's the boss's responsibility, and a very important one.

Everyone needs to be told from time to time how well he is doing. If he has been doing extremely well, he seeks your recognition and praise. He may be anticipating a raise, a promotion, or at least an increase in responsibility. If the employee has been doing poorly, he probably is well aware of it and is concerned about what you may think. He seeks your reassurance, understanding, and support. If he is an average performer, he's probably unsure of your opinion about him. Will it be good, or will it be bad? Employees need to know that average is okay, but that you'd like to see them do better — and think that they *can* do better.

Evaluations are difficult for two reasons: They involve a confrontation of sorts, and they are most often subjective rather than objective.

The process can be far easier — and more beneficial — if:

- You and the employee have previously established certain standards to be met. The employee either has or has not met those standards.
- You concentrate on *performance* and not *personality* during the interview.
- You have established the proper relationship with the employee, i.e., she has been given the opportunity to excel. Whether she has or has not, the choice was her own.
- You use praise as a tool. Even as you point out the employee's weaknesses, failures, and mistakes, you praise him for what he has done and suggest that he can do even better if he will apply himself.

- You think of your role as that of a developmental person, especially when you set performance goals or on-the-job behaviour standards for the employee.
- You do not discuss salaries. Use the interview, instead, as a way to judge performance according to previously agreed standards

After the appraisal interview, you will have to consider the matter of compensation. At that time, base your salary action on:

- The employee's current level of performance.
- The amount of improvement or decline since the employee's last appraisal.
- The way the employee has performed in comparison to others in the same department.
- Market considerations.

No time is more dear to an employee than that during which she is sitting with her employer discussing her performance, discussing her potential for a raise or for a promotion, and (from the employee's point of view) determining whether she has a future with the company or would be better to look elsewhere for employment. These are guarded moments, but both parties will benefit from openness, frankness, and honesty.

DEALING WITH A MARGINAL EMPLOYEE

Realistically, the system is not perfect. We hire the wrong people on occasion. Some people, no matter how promising, do not meet our expectations. People who once seemed to be outstanding suddenly lose their steam and settle into a rut.

The question is, how do you deal with such people?

- Don't act rashly.
- Clarify the individual's goals and the organization's goals.
- Discuss (negotiate) the union of two goals: how the organization can meet the individual's expectations, and how the individual can meet the organization's requirements.

- Maintain your end of the agreement and actively encourage the employee's improvement.
- Constantly monitor the progress being made.
- Use a performance chart or some other record to measure the employee's progress. Be sure the employee has access to it, too, so that he can see how he is doing.
- Recognize that, should all this effort fail to produce an improvement in the employee's performance, it will be time to initiate termination procedures.

HANDLING CHANGE

We already have referred to the inevitability — and the desirability — of change. You must have the foresight to anticipate it and the flexibility to use it to your best advantage.

The best reason to change is to achieve an improvement. There is no value in making a change merely for the sake of it. As the saying goes, 'If it ain't broke, don't fix it'.

Certain warning signs indicate a need for change.

- Awareness that the organization has become over-structured.
- The realization that you are rewarding people for good behaviour, conformity, or tenure rather than for creativity, risk-taking, or productivity.
- The discovery of a lack of communication — upward, downward, and horizontally — within the organization.
- Employee unrest, manifesting itself perhaps in a high rate of turnover.
- Your (or the employees') feelings of confinement, restriction, of being in a rut.
- A falling off of business, or a failure to attract new customers.

Change isn't always welcome, even when it is absolutely necessary. It is only natural that there will be some resistance, and you should be prepared to deal with it when it occurs. These pointers may help:

- Realize that others will not always share your viewpoint, your assessment of the situation, your decision to make a change, or the manner in which you propose to bring about the change.
- Realize too, that other people's beliefs and attitudes often stem from habit and/or lack of information.
- Visualize the change from the viewpoint of those who will be affected by it.
- Anticipate objections, and take steps to counter them.
- Understand that change often triggers tensions and emotions because old behaviour has been shown to be inadequate or because new behaviour may be required.
- Try to bring about change in a slow, smooth manner, not abruptly or disruptively.
- Talk over your plans (and reasons) with key people. If you can get their support before you implement a change, it will make things much easier.
- Keep good channels of communication open with the employees during the period of change.
- Forewarn the employees of the change as early as possible.
- Be willing to bend and modify small points.
- Avoid things that are sure to alienate or agitate the people affected.
- Make trade-offs if they will help to make the situation more acceptable.
- Sell the benefits of the change, not the who, what, and when. (Salespeople often say that they 'sell the sizzle, not the steak'.)

SOLVING PROBLEMS

Probably the most difficult aspect of problem-solving is the feeling of isolation and loneliness that often accompanies it. Pressure builds and tension mounts in direct proportion to the importance of the problem at hand. To ease this pressure, remember one important thing: although you *do* bear the ultimate responsibility, you are *not* alone!

Taking it upon yourself to make the tough decisions is foolish and unnecessary. When you increase the pressure on yourself in this manner, you are increasing the likelihood of making an error, of 'shooting from the hip', of acting on a gut feeling rather than on sound information and solid logic.

Are you alone in a crisis? Not by a long way! We suggest that you consider these allies when faced with solving a critical problem.

- Your solicitor, banker, or accountant.
- Your board of directors and/or key employees.
- Trustworthy suppliers who may have a stake in the outcome of your decision.
- Key customers who also may have a stake in the outcome.
- Even a competitor might help, unless the problem involves them in a direct way.
- Consultants, many of whom offer their services by the hour, the day, or the week.
- Trade or professional associations.
- Business publications — not only in your own field, but in related fields and, for that matter, in any field in which your particular problem may be encountered.
- Other owner managers at the local Small Business Club or Chamber of Commerce.
- Various agencies that have been created specifically to help businesses solve their problems.
- Colleges and universities, which have a significant amount of information, talent, and experience to place at your disposal.

RATING YOUR PROGRESS

Take the time, now and then, to evaluate your progress. How do you rate as a manager?

A healthy bank balance, a respectable P&L statement, and a growing volume of business are all helpful and useful guidelines, to be sure. But go beyond that occasionally. Are you meeting the objectives stated in your business plan? Do you feel in control? Are you personally satisfied with your progress? Do you suffer from any nagging, recurring problems? Have you been able to maintain a satisfying relationship with friends and family outside the office? Do you still have the enthusiasm that you started with? Have you been able to attract and retain good employees? Do you feel that your business has become 'established'? Are you optimistic about your future prospects?

If you can answer all these questions (except the one about 'nagging, recurring problems') in an upbeat, positive manner — without lying to yourself or saying, 'yes, but', then you almost certainly have made it through the difficult start-up period. In the process, you have gained a wealth of experience and self-confidence. You are, as they say, on a roll.

Your task is no longer to *get* going but to *keep* going. Don't lose your momentum!

15
Don't forget your personal life

HANDLING STRESS

As the head of your own business, you should expect to encounter a great deal of stress. Many people do not cope very well with stress, but handling stress is a skill that most people can acquire with some conscious effort.

Lee Trevino, the golfer, has his own definition of stress: 'When you're putting for first place in a $100,000 golf tournament, that's not pressure. When you're playing someone for twenty dollars — and you've got five dollars in your pocket — *that's* pressure!'

To ease stress,

- Allow yourself a margin for error. If your business plan is too finely tuned, a new crisis will develop every time you miss a goal, no matter how minor. Don't build stress into the system; strive to block it out as you make your plan.
- Don't over-extend yourself. We've cautioned against this before, and one reason is to help avoid stress. If you're over-extended, you're bound to be under extra pressure.
- Delegate work. The more you can pass along to others, the less pressure you will then have to bear. Pressure produces stress.
- Realize that no one is perfect. Don't expect it in others, and don't expect it of yourself. There will be times when you will fail; everyone does. Instead of being crushed by the experience, learn from it. Study the situation. Find out

what caused you to fail, and then try again. The key is to fail in the small endeavours and to succeed in the big ones. Savour your accomplishments.

- Don't lose your perspective. Today may be chaos, but tomorrow will be different. Every day, every situation offers a new opportunity, a new challenge, a new reason to be optimistic.
- Build your stamina. Exercise. Eat properly. Get rest. Avoid alcohol and drugs. You will do your best when you feel your best.
- Work at getting some relaxation. Engage in a sport or a hobby. Reading, going to the theatre, or listening to music can be very relaxing. Avoid becoming a workaholic.
- Accept the support of your family and friends. If they don't offer it, ask for it.
- Don't set unreasonable deadlines. Pushing yourself or others only creates stress.
- Don't procrastinate. Putting something off will only make a situation more stressful later on.

When you, as the boss, become burdened by stress, it will spread throughout the organization. People do not do their best work when they are under stress. Get rid of your own tensions, and you will be helping everyone in the firm.

Consider this: a diamond is a chunk of coal that made good under pressure. You can learn to do the same.

COPING WITH FAILURE

Learning to cope with failure is like learning to deal with stress. Stress, after all, is the critical factor in failure.

Everyone experiences failures. The challenge is to learn how to bounce back from a failure and turn the next opportunity into a success.

Nobody scores a thousand in cricket, in business, or in life. If you accept that, you are well on your way to a healthy attitude. Obviously, nobody likes to fail, but if you are afraid to fail, then you will never try the unknown, take a chance, forge a new trail, create new inventions, or reach higher peaks. Fear of failure can be either a great incentive or a formidable barrier for prospective entrepreneurs.

By definition, an entrepreneur is one who undertakes the risk and management of business. And risk implies the possibility of loss or failure.

From childhood on, we are conditioned to win, so losing can be a traumatic experience. But losing also is a learning experience, a broadening experience, a humbling experience. It can heighten one's appreciation of others, enhance one's understanding, soften one's character, and mature one's ego. Winning, on the other hand, can breed arrogance, inflate the ego, and nurture impatience with others. Reality is both winning and losing.

Ask yourself some questions about winning and losing.

- Is it more important for me to *be* right or to *do* right?
- Have I taken a realistic look at my capabilities, or am I planting the seed for my own failure by attempting to do things for which I am not qualified or prepared?
- Am I more concerned about avoiding failure than I am about accomplishing something significant?
- Have I done all I can do to eliminate the obstacles that might prevent success?
- Have I truly failed, or did I give up?
- Am I more concerned about *who's* to blame than *what's* to blame?
- Do I tend to view failure as a form of rejection? Is it — honestly?
- Have I given myself permission to fail now and then? Shouldn't I?
- Do I demand more of myself than I do of others? Is that really fair and sensible?

PACING WORK AND LEISURE

When you make the transition from employee to employer, you're probably going to sacrifice the leisure of a nine-to-five day. That doesn't mean that you should turn into a workaholic.

Workaholics are those who become so obsessed with work

that they allow their lives to get out of balance. They forget the principal purpose of work: to provide a means to sustain a comfortable lifestyle outside the office.

A workaholic lets the puritan ethic run amok, tends to develop a one-track mind, and runs the risk of precluding or destroying personal relationships. To outsiders, he may seem to be inefficient, aloof, or self-centred. In fact, a workaholic actually may be compensating for imaginary shortcomings or simply trying to reaffirm his own sense of importance.

A workaholic is rarely a good team leader and is seldom good at delegating work or responsibility. Often, this stems from fear of taking a risk or fear of competition from others. Although they can be terrific individual performers, the inability of workaholics to work with a team or to delegate frequently means that their overall productivity is low and their likelihood of failure is high.

A workaholic seldom makes a good entrepreneur because success in business calls for the very characteristics that workaholics tend to lack: the ability to create and work with a team, the ability to encourage the participation and co-operation of others, and the ability to accomplish big tasks by dividing them into smaller parts that can be delegated to others.

A successful business person will learn to pace himself. The hours may be irregular, and he may work a greater number of them per week than a salaried employee, but he will not let his work take over his life.

Back away periodically. Relax. Spend time with a hobby. Don't let yourself become so saturated with job-related activities that you lose perspective on your life away from the job.

HOBBIES THAT HEAL

Your time away from the office should refresh your mind, body, and attitude, so that you will have new energy with which to tackle the work ahead. Some people refer to it as 'recharging their battery'.

Deskbound people often get the most out of participating in an outdoor sport, such as golf, tennis, fishing, or hiking, or an outdoor hobby, such as vegetable gardening, flower gardening, or travel.

Travelling people often prefer to relax at home. When this conflicts with the desires of their normally homebound families, they frequently compromise by taking their vacations in a resort-like atmosphere — away from home, yet in a place where they can take root for a period of time.

The so-called 'busman's holiday' seldom provides as much relaxation as a complete departure from one's normal office routine does. Yet even a change of environment can often be very therapeutic. The method of relaxation is not as important as the results it produces.

A number of short breaks may be more relaxing than one long annual holiday. They also may be easier to work in to a busy work schedule.

Even a working vacation — a combination of work and relaxation — can be refreshing. When attending a convention or going on a business trip, extend your stay by a day or two to relax and enjoy the new surroundings.

Being able to delegate your work and responsibilities to others makes it far easier to get away. You can relax a great deal more when there is no need to worry about things going smoothly back at the office.

DIET AND EXERCISE

Matters of diet or exercise are best discussed with your family doctor. But a proper diet and a sufficient amount of exercise will help provide the stamina that is required in the fast-paced, pressure-filled business world.

Grabbing a fast sandwich at your desk or while rushing through an airport terminal is not a good eating habit to get into. Neither is stuffing yourself with rich food while travelling on an expense account or indulging in too many cocktail parties — even with customers. Equally poor is the habit of skipping breakfast or lunch, because your body and mind must be properly nourished if they are to function effectively. Don't sabotage your own system.

Perhaps the easiest thing for a busy individual to ignore is a regular routine of exercise. Time is a precious commodity, and exercise, after all, takes time. A little tennis or squash will consume several hours; a round of golf, half-a-day; fishing or hiking, an entire day.

A common excuse for avoiding exercise is that time not spent in the office is time spent with the family. Members of the family can become quite upset if Mum or Dad is either at the office or on the golf course, but never at home.

Obviously, one way to resolve this situation is to find things that you can do with your family. Encourage your spouse — and your children, if they are old enough — to play golf *with* you. Going swimming or playing football with the kids can be great exercise. Believe it or not, so can doing a number of chores around the house. Instead of getting the kids to mow the lawn, do it yourself if you need the exercise.

Individuals must set a proper diet and a suitable programme of exercise to suit their own needs. Don't ignore them. They are too important to be taken casually.

WORK AT PERSONAL DEVELOPMENT

An entrepreneur must work nearly as hard at developing herself as she does at developing her business. This is particularly true of the individual who never has had any experience in running a business.

New skills must be acquired and honed. A totally different attitude must be developed. Your perspectives must be altered — toward personnel, toward finance, possibly toward business in general. You must think and act like the boss, not one of the gang. Some of these things will come quickly and naturally; others will require hard work and commitment.

The first step is to determine where you need further improvement.

Self-improvement checklist

Which of these items do you need to work on?

_____ Handling correspondence

_____ Developing a good follow-up system
_____ Becoming better organized
_____ Improving your concentration
_____ Making better use of your time
_____ Stopping procrastinating
_____ Becoming a better communicator
_____ Becoming a better listener
_____ Learning to handle pressure and stress
_____ Becoming more sensitive to the needs of others
_____ Developing teamwork
_____ Motivating people
_____ Delegating work and responsibility
_____ Business planning
_____ Understanding finance

Having identified the areas in which you need to develop more skill, put the list in order of priority. Put the skills that you need the most at the top of the list. It may help to write down the reasons why you believe these skills will be important to you.

Now develop an action plan for yourself. Take the first item on your list and write down a number of things that you specifically intend to do and bring about the desired change. Also write down the date by which you will do each of those things and the results that you expect to achieve by doing them.

Your action plan will look something like this:

A   *Reasons for making the improvement*
    1
    2
    3
    4

B   *Specific steps to be taken (give a date)*
    1   by _____
    2   by _____
    3   by _____

C   *Results expected (give a date)*
    1   by _____
    2   by _____
    3   by _____

Do this for every item on your list. Be realistic when you set dates and specify the results expected. Don't be too demanding of yourself. Only you will judge the outcome.

You will find that meeting realistic deadlines and achieving realistic goals will stimulate you to work harder at self-improvement, whereas the disappointment of missing unrealistic targets will only tend to discourage you and impede your progress.

FOUNDERS CAN'T BE KEEPERS

Almost from the moment you start a new business, you will begin to give it away, piece by piece, day by day. Get used to the idea.

The objective of every business enterprise is growth, and growth involves constant change. You cannot grow while standing still. Or, as one philosopher phrased it, 'There's only one direction in which to coast — downhill'.

As the business grows, you will have to delegate more work to more people. In doing so, you will be giving up portions of your personal work and individual authority.

As the growth continues, you probably will need more money, which may involve taking in partners or selling shares. Once again, you will have to sacrifice some of your responsibility, some of your independence, some of your individuality, perhaps even some of your ownership position.

Many entrepreneurs find this hard to do. Some go as far as to limit the growth of their business so that it will not exceed their personal limitations. In the long run, this is not a wise decision for a number of reasons.

- It makes the company too dependent on a single individual. If anything should happen to that individual, the firm could collapse.
- It limits your earning potential rather than expanding it. This also means that it limits the growth potential, both economically and professionally, of your employees. In time, you may begin to lose your most important people.
- By limiting your growth, you are opening the door to competition. In time, the competition may outgrow you and take over your business.

The more you attempt to hang on to the business, the more you may be retarding its growth. Learn to let go — carefully, cautiously — so that the company, the employees, and you will have the freedom and flexibility to expand. Together, you can achieve a great deal more than any individual could ever expect to achieve alone.

Part IV

Growing the business

16
Prepare for growth

The questions we encouraged you to answer at the end of Chapter 15 were a way to suggest that, at a given stage in almost every business, one can expect to reach a turning point.

The preplanning is over, the business has been launched, and the company has, if not matured, at least reached its adolescence. Suddenly, often without a great deal of forewarning, you may encounter another very critical crossroad. Let's call it the 'turning point', because it is at this juncture that the business will continue to grow, will flatten out on a plateau, or will begin to decline.

A number of things can trigger such a turning point.

- *The need to expand.* A restaurant needs more seating capacity. A manufacturer needs another or a larger factory. A retailer wants to add one or more additional stores. The business needs to expand its product line. There is an opportunity to buy out a competitor.
- *Your initial market becomes saturated.* There are no more customers for your product or service. To gain more business, you must increase your product line or expand into another geographic area. Your factory is producing at maximum capacity. Your restaurant is serving as many people as it can accommodate.
- *Your product or service is growing obsolete.* The initial product or service was seasonal, and there is a need to generate during the off-season. The restaurant originally was located at a prime traffic intersection, but a new bypass has rerouted all of the traffic. The initial product or

service caught on as a fad, but the novelty is beginning to wear off (for example, the companies that once manufactured deely boppers). A new technology has outdated your product or service (for example, the firms that once produced valves for the electronics field).

You will notice that the same problem may suggest several different solutions. The restaurant owner, for example, may:

- Continue doing business as usual.
- Expand the present restaurant to provide more seating.
- Move the business to another, larger facility.
- Keep the restaurant and open another one at a second location.

Obviously, the growth of the restaurant suggests choosing one of the last three options. If the owner chooses to continue doing business as usual, further growth will be impossible and the business will either plateau or begin to decline. It also is obvious, however, that each of the growth options entails a certain degree of risk — not unlike that which the owner had to overcome when the business first got started.

For the individual who started a business from scratch and who does not have a great deal of working capital, there is now an additional problem to face: will a change in the entire business structure be required in order to finance the anticipated growth?

Assume our restaurateur went into business as a sole proprietor. Now, although the business is showing a nice profit, there is the need for a large amount of money either to remodel and expand; locate a new site, remodel and move; or locate, remodel, equip, and establish a second restaurant. Does the owner go heavily into debt and borrow the money? Or take in a partner and convert the business to a partnership? Or incorporate and sell shares to various investors?

Whatever the course of action, this is a major turning point for the business. The owner decides that the business is doing well and ought to be left alone, or goes into debt, perhaps even deeper than when the business first started, or relinquishes a part of the business to a partner or to a number of shareholders. Having once taken on the responsibility of a large debt, the thought of taking on even more debt is difficult to accept. On the other hand, the acquisition of a partner may not be very attractive, either. Selling shares in a company may be safer and less restricting, and there would be some considerable tax benefits associated with incorporation. Perhaps incorporating is the way to go. Perhaps not.

These are the mechanics of coming to a decision at the business's turning point. The questions are serious, complex, and may alter the original framework of the company's structure. They certainly are real and difficult — if not impossible — to avoid.

Hopefully, the skills that you have acquired since going into business will see you through this crisis. Certainly, personality plays a role. For the person with a modest ego and moderate aspirations, a 'nice little business' may be adequate. On the other hand, if the person is highly motivated, highly ambitious, and determined to build the business into the largest enterprise possible, then that individual might have to bite the bullet and press on.

There may be a number of these turning points in the growth and expansion of a business. Most probably, the first will be the most traumatic because it will hit you when you are the least experienced and, in all likelihood, the most undecided about what you would like your company to become. If you opt to stay small and be conservative at the first juncture, for example, you may never be faced with another opportunity of this type. If you opt for growth and fail, you could lose everything that you have worked for to this point. And if you opt for growth and succeed, similar turning points may recur again and again.

In modern business, a new type of enterprise is emerging — call it *acquisition*. A company that has available capital will seek out other profitable companies and buy them as an investment. The economics are simple: a thriving company will pay a higher rate of return (including tax benefits) than most other types of investment, and furthermore, the diversification can be an excellent hedge against a recession or a depression. Often, the cross-pollination between the two companies is also advantageous (as, for example, when a TV network acquires a film-producing company).

We cannot advise you, in a book such as this, on which course to pursue in these situations. There are far too many variables.

We *can* suggest that you surround yourself with the most capable financial and legal advisers available and that you follow the course that is the most advantageous to *you*.

Having said as much, let us address the problems of those who have started a business and who are (at least, to this point) *not* at a turning point in their business lives. They simply wish to see their business grow and prosper.

John Cowan
Trend Trophies, Ltd

John Cowan scored a bullseye when he took on Keith Harrison as General Manager. Cowan is the owner of Trend Trophies, Ltd, a Newcastle-based firm making sports trophies. John had started the business in 1980 and it had grown quite quickly, but once he reached a staff of about 20, growth stopped and everything seemed hard work.

John says, 'This trade is all to do with fads and fashions. Every year we have to do something different from our competitors and be able to spot trends. As long as we manage to bring out our designs first then we are achieving what we set out to do'. The trouble was that John was spending too much time running around in circles trying to do everything, instead of tackling the strategic developments and using his creative skills to design innovative trophies.

Keith Harrison, on the other hand, was a professional manager who had spent all his career in large firms. Keith was introduced to Trend Trophies during a retraining programme at a local business school. John Cowan needed a manager, but didn't know it, Keith needed the experience of a smaller firm to widen his horizons. The match was perfect. After three months, Keith was appointed as General Manager.

John admitted that although he 'adopted a strict common-sense approach to the financial side' he was 'doing it without knowing what he was doing'. Now they know exactly where they are. They have a clear financial structure and targets. They have a well-managed production unit and John is free to take the business over the £1m mark and into another league.

BECOMING A MORE EFFECTIVE LEADER

There are significant differences between being the head of a new firm and being the head of an established, proven, tested company. As the former, you are viewed as a newcomer, perhaps even as an interloper or an upstart. As the latter, you have established your business qualifications, filed your credentials, and become something of a force in the market-place.

You have gained experience and confidence. You have a reliable personal income and a steady cash flow to sustain your business. You have achieved a professional reputation and a financial reputation. You have earned the support of your suppliers, your customers, and your employees.

Where once you were an unknown quantity, you now have a track record on which to stand and by which others may judge you.

Ask yourself:

- Am I financially secure, at least for the moment?
- Do I have the opportunity to be creative?
- Do I have time for myself? My family? My friends?
- Am I in good health?

The ultimate question is, how much are you willing to sacrifice for success? Another £100,000? Another three hours at the office each day? Another five years before the company becomes what you would like it to be?

Do you feel satisfied and secure with what you have achieved so far? Do you want more? Are you willing to do what it will take to achieve more?

Particularly if the risks are small, most entrepreneurs hope that the business they have founded will continue to grow. There is more satisfaction in developing a large business than in running a small one. There is more recognition, more prestige, and of course, more money.

By and large, most people hate the thought of being called a quitter. They like to see a project through to its conclusion. Like a gambler, they thrill to the excitement of turning the next card, playing the odds, betting on their own talent and judgement.

This, after all, is what drew them into business in the first place. Unless the cost is too great, there is little reason for them to change.

As your business grows, however, the challenges to your business acumen will grow. Small decisions will become big decisions. Matters involving a few people will become matters involving dozens, even hundreds of people. Cash considerations that began in the thousands of pounds will escalate to the tens of thousands and perhaps hundreds of thousands of pounds. Talents with which you entered business may no longer suffice. Where will you go for the additional expertise?

RATE YOURSELF A LEADER

Realistically evaluating your personal strengths and weaknesses is a worthwhile exercise. You are not the same person that you were when you first went into business. You have learned new skills and acquired a great deal of firsthand experience. Through the process of critical self-evaluation, you have repeatedly isolated certain areas in which you were weak and have worked to overcome those weaknesses. You have learned new ways to capitalize on your greatest strengths. You have learned to use your organization to provide many of the things that you could not personally offer to the business, such as legal expertise, perhaps.

What kind of leader are you today?

You are still stronger in some areas than in others. Are there ways to take greater advantage of those strengths?

There are still certain areas in which you could use some improvement. What are you doing to overcome those weaknesses? For added emphasis, repeat the self-rating checklist on pages 216-17.

Do you have solid, well-trained, experienced, and competent people in every key position in the company? Or have you surrounded yourself with those who are merely loyal? Have you taken the steps necessary to clear out the deadwood? Have you taken the steps to see that people will be ready to take over the key positions when the time comes?

Have you reviewed your business plan regularly? How has it

changed from your original business plan? Is some sort of trend beginning to emerge?

Are you satisfied with the company's financial performance? Are there ways you could reduce costs, increase income, improve cash flow, or increase profits?

Are your employees satisfied with their work? Are they enthusiastic and productive? Do you have a normal rate of turnover — or better? Is your salary structure competitive?

Have you created the proper channels of communication to ensure a fast, accurate flow of information? Or do you feel that you might be losing control? Do you communicate downward throughout the organization, or simply expect others to keep *you* informed?

Have you established a good relationship with your suppliers? Could you count on their support if some unusual circumstance were to occur?

Have you evaluated your customers' satisfaction? Are you getting a great deal of repeat business, or is it necessary to constantly seek out new customers? Have you analysed why?

Are the daily pressures diminishing or increasing? Have you over-extended? Have you failed to delegate sufficiently or wisely enough?

IMPROVING THE WORKFORCE

Since the quality of a company's personnel is critical in the success or failure of the organization, the task of hiring, training, and retaining good people never ends.

You can't expect to have a perfect record. Some of your people will fail to meet your expectations. Get rid of them, or at least, assign them to responsibilities where their less-than-desirable performance won't hurt you. Be careful that their mediocrity does not infect the rest of your personnel. If marginal employees fail to gain salary increases or promotions, they will probably resign eventually. Maybe they will learn a lesson and become balls of fire on their next jobs. Some of your top performers may have been duds in earlier positions.

The important thing is to search for excellence, reward excellence, and constantly strive to create excellence.

How do you search for excellence? You begin with a clear understanding of what it is that you're looking for. Make a list of the responsibilities that you want the new employee to assume. From that, make a list of the qualifications a candidate must have in order to handle those responsibilities. Use quantitative terms — level of education, years of experience, and so on. Also make a list of any qualifications that you might prefer the candidate to have, assuming all the other qualifications have been met.

As you interview each candidate, eliminate anyone who doesn't possess all the 'must' qualifications. Those are absolute minimum requirements for the person you seek to hire, and you should not employ anyone who falls short of them. (But don't list so many qualifications that the list is unduly — and unnecessarily — restrictive.) Primarily, you are seeking to find the candidates who stand the greatest likelihood of doing the job successfully and to weed out any candidates who, in all probability, will not do well because they lack the basic tools to do the job.

If there are several candidates who satisfy the list of 'musts', use your list of 'prefers' to complete the selection process.

The past is a good indication of the future. A person who has had a good track record over the years is a much better candidate than a person with a patchy record. One of the things you should be looking for is consistency. (Although there are those who seriously question the value of one's past performance as an indication of how that individual will perform in the future, one thing is incontestable: it is easier to maintain motivation in a person than it is to create it.) Study the candidate's personality as well as his or her capabilities. Will the candidate fit in with the organization? Will the candidate be a good team worker? Someone who is less qualified in, say, education or experience is more likely to succeed than someone who is a personality misfit.

During the interview, make liberal use of the question, 'Why?'

- Why did you leave your last job?
- Why did you say that?
- Why would you do that?
- Why do you feel that way?

Facts can be extracted from a candidate's CV or job application and verified with past employers or other sources. The purpose of the interview is to develop information that is not on the CV to explore the candidate's personality and judgement, to uncover the candidate's flaws and weaknesses (which no candidate will put on a CV).

The latter can be particularly valuable to you in making a selection. An employer does not wish to encounter any surprises after a person has been hired. If the candidate has some weaknesses, the time to uncover them is during the interview, before you offer the person the job. If they are serious flaws, you don't want the individual in your firm, and the individual probably would not be successful if he were.

Some other tips about screening job applicants:

- Keep the candidate talking by avoiding questions that can be answered with a simple yes or no.
- Although it is important to put the candidate at ease, don't waste time with a lot of idle small talk.
- Don't be afraid to ask a potentially embarrassing question:
    1 Why were you out of work for six months?
    2 Were you let go by that company or did you resign? Why?
    3 What were the things that you disliked about your last job?
- Seek people who can compensate for your weaknesses.
- Look for hard workers, not clock watchers.
- Watch for high achievers with a strong desire to succeed.
- Hire intelligent people who have the capacity to learn and grow in your company.
- Look for people who tend to be independent but not dogmatic. Avoid anyone who seems to be insecure or uncertain.
- Do not allow the candidate to rely on the word *we*. You want to know what the candidate can do, not what a previous team of people could do.
- Avoid discussing the particulars of the job you have available until the end of the interview. Then ask if the candidate has questions about the position. Saying too much at the beginning will give the candidate an opportunity to slant the answers he gives you. The type of questions that the candidate asks about the job will tell you a great deal about

his orientation to the position — salary, security, growth potential, and so on.

Perhaps you have delegated the responsibility for screening and hiring new personnel to someone else. Once a company reaches a certain size, it is almost impossible for the chief executive to handle this job personally (although most chief executives still play an active role when it comes to hiring people for key positions).

Assuming that you have delegated — or will one day delegate — this responsibility to another person, avoid interfering. If you are asked for an opinion, give one, but make it clear that you are not making the final decision. If you have delegated that responsibility to someone else, that person should be allowed to make the decisions — and should be held accountable for them.

Having done your best to hire good people, how do you encourage their growth and channel that growth in a direction that will be of most benefit to the company?

A good starting point would be to concentrate on those things that the individual can do, rather the things he can't do. Evaluate your people regularly and try to determine two things about each one. What are the individual's strengths? And what additional strengths could be developed, given a little time, training, and encouragement?

Discuss these evaluations with the employee. Comment on her strengths and describe the areas in which she could develop new skills. Explain why it would be to her benefit — as well as the company's — to do so. Assure the individual of your support and show her how she can acquire the skill(s) in question. Find out if she is really interested in developing the recommended skills, and if so, offer her your encouragement.

Follow-through is important. See if the employee pursues the self-improvement programme that you have discussed. Keep an eye on her performance. Praise all signs of improvement, and provide fresh encouragement any time there seems to have been some setback. Be particularly supportive if the improvements make an impact on the individual's work for the company.

Through this process, helping to develop each individual in the organization, your people will:

● Broaden their perspective regarding the goals and objectives of the company.

- Increase their individual and collective capabilities.
- Do their work better.
- Be able to be of more help to others with whom they work.
- Be happier and more highly motivated.
- Be encouraged to be more independent, more innovative, more self-reliant, more resourceful, and more creative.

With such a pool of talent from which to draw, you should rarely have to look outside the company when positions of greater responsibility open up. Neither should you have to worry about the potential loss of key people, because you can be assured that there are competent replacements waiting for an opportunity. (It almost goes without saying that your key people also will recognize this fact — a realization that ought to keep them on their toes.)

Some other thoughts regarding employee and organization development:

- Remember that employee development is not a one-way street. A company helps an individual to grow so that he is better equipped to help the company grow. Be sure the employee understands this symbolic relationship, too.
- Encourage your key people — and other employees as well — to be active participants in this concept, helping each other gain new skills and assume greater responsibility whenever the opportunities present themselves.
- Never allow any suggestion of favouritism, bias, or prejudice to interfere with this programme. Opportunities should be made available to each and every individual in the company.
- Use the concept as an incentive — and even as a reward, on occasion — but never withhold an opportunity for self-improvement in order to punish.
- Be particularly mindful of developing those who have the potential to acquire skills that will be most valuable to the company.
- A new skill, once acquired, will atrophy if it is not put to use. Once an employee has acquired a new skill, give him a chance to use it.
- Do not view it as a loss when an employee that you have been developing resigns from the company. Presumably, the grooming did produce some benefits for the organiza-

tion, and one day the employee may even return. In any event, one disappointment is hardly proof that the concept is a failure. Count your successes, not your failures.

- Believing in your business and approaching it enthusiastically is contagious. Spread this contagion throughout your organization.
- Keep your people involved in growing the business. When they have ideas, listen to them. In 1932, 191 members of the National Association of Suggestion Systems reported that employee suggestions had saved them a cumulative total of $700 million — a return of $6 for every dollar they invested in such programmes!
- Keep the employees working toward common goals. The shortest distance between two points is a straight line.
- Delegate responsibility to demonstrate your trust in the employees, to encourage independent thinking, to increase an employee's pride, increase an employee's self-reliance.
- Tap this resource as a way to help the company solve problems and make decisions.
- Let everyone know that all of the jobs in your company are important. No one should ever feel that the work she is doing is insignificant or inconsequential.

Certainly, no one should ever ignore the importance of salary as a way to develop an organization. Although salary alone is not enough to satisfy your employees, as we already have noted, it most surely is one of their major considerations.

It is as unrealistic to think that one can go out an buy a complete team of good employees as it is to believe that a company can retain a good team of people and not be economically competitive. So we must concede that money *can* be used to inspire and motivate employees, while still acknowledging that employees are not motivated solely by money and that such things as professional growth, interesting work, and sympathetic management cannot be ignored.

How, then, to use salary most effectively as a tool for increasing productivity and company growth?

The most frequently used technique (and the least effective, in our opinion) is the rise. Salary increases have become too automatic in business, and people have become accustomed to getting rises simply for doing an average job. Therefore, if we expect to get something beyond that, we really are talking about an 'extraordinary' rise. But with that, you are running the risk of alienating other employees, setting a poor precedent, and creating a false standard by which an employee can judge his future performance.

It is better, in our opinion, to offer an incentive that is well understood before the fact, that is tied to specific standards of performance, and that is virtually uncontestable by the other workers.

I recall one company, a publishing firm, that paid its advertising salespeople a commission. The chief executive officer of that company told me one day that he planned to reduce the territory of his top performer. I asked 'Why? Is it too much for him to handle?'

'No', the CEO replied, 'but I just realized that this guy is making more money than I am!'

'Perhaps he's drawing a bigger salary than you are', I countered, 'but you own the company! Every pound he makes represents eight pounds that he's making for you!'

The CEO had never looked at the situation in that light. Happily for all concerned, the CEO allowed his top salesman to retain his territory and increase his sales — as well as his income. Both the salesman and the company prospered.

That is the essence of a profit-sharing incentive. Such programmes are easier to create for salesmen and certain other types of employee than they are for others, but they can be used as an effective motivational tool for virtually any type of job. On the assembly or production line, profit-sharing would involve a salary plus an incentive based on exceeding a specified quota. In nonproducing departments, it would involve a bonus for exceeding specified minimum standards of performance, such as reducing costs, speeding deliveries, minimizing customer complaints, reducing stock.

Any department may be considered a profit (or loss) component of the company, and incentives may be established to reward those who contribute to increasing that profit (or reducing the loss).

One company set up a programme that worked like this: An incentive fund was created amounting to 15 per cent of the company's profits. That fund was then divided among the employees according to their percentage of the total company payroll, and each employee was evaluated as unsatisfactory (no bonus), satisfactory (basic bonus), or excellent (double the basic bonus).

Assume the company has 1,500 employees and produces £5 million in pre-incentive profits. Fifteen per cent of £5 million is £750,000, and that is the amount that was put into the incentive fund.

Of the 1,500 employees, 100 are rated unsatisfactory, 1,250 are rated satisfactory, and 150 are rated excellent. Since unsatisfactory employees do not benefit from the fund, they go uncounted. The satisfactory group of 1,250 are awarded a single credit, and the excellent group of 150 are awarded two credits each — a total of 1,550 credits (1,250 + 300 = 1,550).

The 1,550 credits are divided into the £750,000 incentive fund, giving each credit a value of approximately £418.

Satisfactory employees, then, receive a bonus of £418, and excellent employees receive a bonus of £836.

The point is, this is a plan that recognizes the employees' contributions to the company and rewards those employees according to the level of their contribution.

Some other thoughts about the use of incentive compensation:

- The bonus cheque should be presented to the employee by the individual who has performed the employee's evaluation. The superior should use this occasion to compliment the employee on her performance, encourage the employee to strive equally hard in the future, and suggest ways in which the employee can improve.

  The superior should use equal diplomacy with those who do not receive a bonus, explaining why and explaining exactly what the employee must do in order to receive a bonus the next year.
- You should be sure that the employees are evaluated fairly and consistently. A tough supervisor or manager might recommend very few employees for a bonus, while a more lenient one might recommend far too many. If this sort of situation is allowed to occur, the entire programme would be in jeopardy. Dissent could arise, interdepartmental squabbling could occur, and widespread dissatisfaction could result.

This is only one way to use money as an employee incentive. There are a great many others, and you should select one that will help you to accomplish your own purposes.

Employee incentives are not a form of largesse; they are a way to stimulate employees to exceptional, perhaps even extraordinary, levels of performance. Be sure you receive what you are paying for.

Do not reward such things as tenure, loyalty, and punctuality. Do not reward an employee who is simply doing the job that he was hired to do. Reward those who have exceeded the anticipated level of performance and those for whom you can anticipate a more prominent role in your organization.

GETTING NEW BUSINESS

The success of any business means growth, and growth can mean different types of businesses. A firm may grow, for example, by:

- Doing more business with existing customers.
- Attracting new customers.
- Raising its prices.
- Expanding its line of products or services.
- Buying out a competitor.

Some of these are available to one type of business and not to another. A restaurant, for example, can increase its business by adding more tables. A dress shop cannot increase its business simply by putting more dresses on the racks, but it might increase its business by adding a line of men's or children's wear. A retailer or a manufacturer might lose business by trying to raise prices, but an architect or a hair stylist might be able to do it. A pub can't expect to increase its business by drawing customers from a faraway town, but a manufacturer or a building contractor might very well expand his business into other regions.

There also are different patterns of growth.

A retailer, for example, might choose the *horizontal* pattern — grow from one store to two, to three, and so on.

The same retailer might, on the other hand, decide to choose a *vertical* growth pattern — from the operation of several stores to becoming a wholesaler, and then to becoming a manufacturer.

As a variation on both of those, the retailer might decide on a pattern of *diversification* — from selling women's apparel to selling clothing for the entire family, to adding shoes and accessories, to becoming a full-scale department store.

Whatever the manner of growth, chances are it will require additional personnel. Hence our emphasis on the need to hire, train, and retain good people in your business. If a restaurant adds more tables, it will probably need more waiters, buspersons, and kitchen help. If a dress shop adds a new line, it will probably need more salespeople. If a manufacturer or a contractor branches out into other states, he probably will need more salespeople, office help, and work crews.

One should plan for growth. Hire and train the necessary personnel in advance. Add new equipment in advance. Most of all, budget in advance for the cost of expansion.

It takes money to underwrite growth, and it is far better to have funds set aside for that purpose than it is to have to borrow it from a bank.

Be wary of rapid growth. Obviously, you must seize an opportunity when it presents itself, but avoid spreading yourself too thinly. Avoid acting in haste. Get the best advice available, both from inside and outside the organization.

Look at the hole, and not the doughnut. The benefits may be more obvious than the drawbacks, and they may tend to cloud your judgement. Ask yourself, 'What would this really cost me?' Then ask, 'Is it worth it?'

I know of one businessman who started a small manufacturing company and built it into a company of some size. In time, a major corporation bought the firm for several million dollars, but discovered that it lacked adequate management expertise. After several years, several changes of management, and a considerable decline in sales and profits, the big corporation sold the business back to the original founder for a fraction of what they'd paid to buy it. Under its original ownership, the company began to flourish again.

Quite obviously, my friend has prospered very nicely from this double transaction. However, the other corporation suffered a loss of several millions!

If your plans for growth include the acquisition of another business, you would do well to keep this story in mind. Success in business is often comparable to a game of Monopoly, except that the money involved is real. In business, as in Monopoly, there are winners, and there are losers.

DEVELOPING NEW PRODUCTS

Often the opportunity to grow depends on the introduction of new products or services. The product or service on which you originally based the business may become obsolete. The market may get saturated. Competitors may enter the field and erode your profitability.

Virtually every product goes through a fairly predictable life cycle. The product is introduced, it enjoys a growth in sales and acceptance, it matures, and then it begins to decline. Typically, sales continue to increase until the product reaches maturity. Profits, however, begin to decline as soon as the product has passed its growth cycle.

It is during the time when a product is enjoying its greatest growth — a time when both sales and profits are rising — that the company should begin to think about new product development.

A number of years ago, the Addressograph-Multigraph Corporation (now known as AM International) had two very successful and very profitable products on the market. The Addressograph is a system by which names and addresses (or other data) are stamped onto small metal plates. These plates are used throughout the world for maintaining mailing lists and other files. Dog tags containing the name, serial number, and blood type of each person in military service were produced by the million on Addressograph plates. Today's credit cards are really a plastic variation of the Addressograph plate.

The Multigraph is a small, inexpensive type of printing press. Unlike the traditional printing equipment of the time, however, the Multigraph does not require the use of type. An original document is fed into the machine, which transfers the image onto a paper or metal 'master' and then reproduces that image onto standard-size precut paper at a high rate of speed.

Both machines were excellent products and produced billions of dollars' worth of sales for Addressograph-Multigraph. Unfortunately, management believed that its good fortune would last forever. Products of equal marketability were not developed and produced.

The rest of the story is probably apparent already. The use of electronic computers virtually wiped out the market for the Addressograph; and the development of the photocopier captured most of the market previously enjoyed by Multigraph. Complacency has destroyed more than one company. New product development cannot be ignored.

Realize that a new product does not necessarily mean a new technology or a revolutionary new concept. Consider the changes that have taken place over the years regarding some very common household items:

Table 8

Product development

Product	'New' development
Toothpaste	Powders, pastes, and gels
	Different colours
	Different flavours
	Pump dispensers, metal and plastic tubes
	Cavity-fighting additives
	Plaque-fighting additives
	Special formulations for denture wearers
	Special formulations for smokers
	Special formulations for people with sensitive gums
Beer	Different methods of brewing
	'Light' formulations
	Low-alcohol formulations
	Bottles of various sizes
	Cans of various sizes
	Draught and pasteurized
	Six-packs and eight-packs
	Pop-tops and screw-off tops

Cigarettes	Standard, king, and extra long
	Flavours
	Aromatics
	Filtered and unfiltered
	Papers and various colours
	Products targeted towards women
	Packages, boxes, and tins
	Packs of twenty and twenty-five
	Cigarette-size cigars
	Non-tobacco cigarettes
Milk	Homogenized
	Pasteurized
	Glass bottles, plastic bottles, and cartons
	Pints, quarts, half-gallons, and gallons
	High fat and low fat
	Flavoured
	Powdered
	Vitamin-fortified
Soap	Bars, flakes, powders, and liquids
	Various sizes and shapes
	Various scents
	Various colours
	With moisturizing cream
	For men and for women
	With a string to hang around your neck in the shower
	As a gift item in boutiques
	As souvenirs
	For pets and animals

Every new development begins with a new idea. Most ideas are impractical, impossible, too dangerous, or too expensive, but some ideas filter through to reach the market.

Some products result from a combination of two or more ideas: The clock-radio. The wristwatch that tells not only the time but the day, the date, and possibly a number of other things, too.

In 1911, one avid hunter and outdoorsman got tired of coming home with wet, soggy leather boots. His solution was a boot with leather tops for support and rubber feet for protection against the water. That was the beginning of L.L. Bean — a company now doing about $250 million a year in sales.

Ideas come from questions.

- What would happen if. . .?
- Why don't we. . .?
- Wouldn't it be nice if there were something to. . .?
- Why hasn't somebody. . .?
- What can we do to. . .?
- How can I. . .?

The development of a new product is a process. You begin by asking questions. From the answers to those questions, you get ideas. From the ideas comes a period of further questioning, testing, experimenting, and even some failing. And then the emergence of a new product.

Few of us have the mind of a Thomas Edison. We need help developing ideas. Ask your employees. Ask your customers, 'What do you need that isn't currently available?' (Sounds simplistic? Perhaps simpler than you think. For example, Barber to customer: 'What do you need that isn't currently available?' Customer: 'Something that would grow hair on my head.' 'Product idea — a hair restorer.)

Since the 1920s, 3M has allowed its researchers to spend 15 per cent of their time on any new project that interests them. Over the years, this has led to a number of new products, including their current top-seller, 'Post-It Notes'.

Study the new technologies and the new products that other people are introducing to the market. Ask yourself, 'Is there some way in which that could help me?' For example, Velcro is now replacing laces in shoes; buttons and zippers on jackets; glue and other adhesives on a number of products. It's even being used to unite the two halves of the Jarvick artificial heart! Baking powder, long a standard item in everybody's kitchen, is now being marketed as a way to remove odours from the refrigerator and even as a compound to use in cleaning rugs.

During World War II, when our traditional sources of rubber were cut off, there was a mad scramble to see if someone could produce a synthetic rubber. Many things were tried, including the sap of the milkweed.

One laboratory produced a substance that, although not suitable as a synthetic rubber, did have a number of unusual qualities. You could shape it like clay, but if you put it down, it would melt back down into a puddle. It could be rolled into a ball that would bounce like rubber, but if you froze it and struck it with a hammer, it would shatter like glass. The product was just another laboratory oddity, until someone looked at it as something other than an attempt to make artificial rubber that failed.

The imaginative individual created an eye-catching egg-shaped plastic container for the substance, called it Potty Putty, and made a fortune.

Mark Twain once remarked, 'The man with a new idea is a crank — until the idea succeeds.'

Not every idea will succeed; but as the Potty Putty example illustrates, there are many more ideas in the world than there are people who have the imagination to recognize them. In all probability, there is no such thing as a bad idea. One person's failure could be the beginning of another's fortune.

WHAT SERVICE REALLY MEANS

'All right,' you say to yourself, 'it's one thing to develop and manufacture a new product, but I deal in service, and that's a totally different ballgame.'

Different, perhaps — but not totally different. The question-to-idea-to-solution process is the same.

- What service do people want or need?
- What things do people dislike to do for themselves?
- What things can we do better (faster, cheaper) than people can do for themselves?

Like many people, a woman in California hesitated to entrust her small child to the care of a young girl — the only babysitter available in the neighbourhood. One day, the newspaper carried a story that told how a group of young children had visited a retirement home in the community to sing for the people residing there. The article was accompanied by photographs, and a glance at the expressions on the faces of the residents of the retirement home clearly indicated how much they had enjoyed the children's performance. 'How much pleasure they can receive by being around children,' the California mother thought.

The next day, the mother took her child to the retirement home and asked if any of the residents would be interested in babysitting. 'I can provide the transportation to pick you up and get you back,' she added. A number of residents volunteered.

The young mother had an idea. She visited other retirement homes, where she received the same enthusiastic response, She placed an ad in the newspaper, asking if other elderly people would be interested in babysitting. They would.

This imaginative young California mother now operates a thriving business that rents 'grandparents' to families that are in need of babysitting services.

In this case, the enterprising California mother tapped the community's elderly as a source of staff. The elderly are also a major market for those in the service business. According to the Census Bureau, there are now over 25 million people over the age of sixty-five in America — and the number increases by 1,500 persons each day! By the year 2050, it is estimated that 67 million people — one in four — will be over sixty-five.

An enterprising student from Liverpool, typically short of spending money, realized that he could save his friends a lot of time in job hunting. He offered the service of fact finding on prospective employers, digging out information which the firms would not publicize themselves. When his clients went for interview they were suitably impressive; well informed and could ask difficult questions!

Sometimes, it seems, certain firms forget that they are in the service business. A restaurant, for example, is a service business. Restaurants do not sell food; groceries sell food. Restaurants provide the service of preparing food, serving food, and cleaning up afterward. Successful restaurants never lose sight of the difference.

As the name implies, a service business should provide a convenience for the customer. Is there anyone who has not rankled at a painter who leaves the house in a shambles? A plumber who leaves to get a part and doesn't show up again for three days? A rude waiter? A snooty desk clerk? A slovenly cab driver?

This is not to deprecate all painters, plumbers, waiters, desk clerks, or cab drivers. I had my house redone recently by a painter who was absolutely immaculate — but it was a different painter from the one I mentioned in the last paragraph. And that's the whole point: people do not go back to a business that has treated them badly.

With society enjoying a comfortable level of affluence, with the growing number of people over sixty-five, with the increase of single-parent households, with the continuing trend toward two-income families, and with the tremendous increase in working women, the opportunities to provide service are greater than ever. Seek them out. Be innovative. Be resourceful, and you can seize one of those opportunities for your own.

17
Prepare for the future

Going into business is not a whimsical proposition. The short term benefits are often few, although the long term benefits may be substantial. Few entrepreneurs can or will get rich quick. Long-range planning includes consideration not only of the company's future but of the employee's future, your own future and the future of your family as well.

As with most companies, there is a need to plan for succession — who is going to take over? When a key employee resigns, retires or dies, there must be an employee who is trained, experienced and capable of taking the other's place. Your own position is not exempt from such a consideration. Who will be capable, one day, of taking your place?

The main ways open to you of meeting your responsibilities and reaping your just rewards are to sell out, to pass on ownership to your children or employees, or to go public. It is possible to do all three! If your business is too small to pass on, or if nobody else wants it, then your reward can come from the sale of the assets and the business name and from a well-planned pension fund for yourself.

The recently retired owner of a small chain of supermarkets says that in order to plan the sale of the business properly he started to think of the business as a *product* itself. He brought in a design firm to give the shops an up to date image, he trained the management team in the latest technology and he improved efficiency to competitors' standards. He then analysed the market by looking for competitors and other regional chains with 'gaps' which his business could fill.

As a result of the analysis, he came up with a handful of

potential buyers who would benefit from owning his stores. He put together a business proposal, saying what the benefits were and approached his 'prospects'. The result was a sale to a chain of stores looking for expansion by acquisition. The sale price was around £8m. A year later the business was devalued by £2m, because the true value was deemed to be nearer £6m. The £2m bonus was the result of 'good marketing' of the product!

If you sell or dispose of your business or shares in it, you will be liable for capital gains tax. However, there is considerable tax relief available if you are retiring after the age of sixty or because of ill health.

As long as you have been the owner-manager and a working director for over a year you are eligible for tax relief on the capital gains from the sale or transfer of shares in the business. If you have been in that position for ten years you can get the full relief available, currently full exemption on the first £125,000 and 50 per cent exemption on gains between £125,000 and £500,000.

If you plan to leave the business or your profits to someone else, then plan well ahead. Inheritance tax is currently 40 per cent of all transfers above £110,000. You can make lifetime transfers of £3,000 a year tax free, but these will be taxed if you die less than seven years after making the transfer.

EVALUATE YOUR RETIREMENT OPTIONS

So that you can plan productively, you should consider the eventuality of your retirement. You must have people who are trained and capable to take your place in the business, or perhaps have a plan to liquidate your holdings. You must have an adequate financial plan to sustain you for the rest of your life.

What is the best time to retire? Simple answers, such as 'when you're 65' or 'whenever you've got enough money' aren't satisfactory. Neither is the prospect of hanging on until you're no longer capable of doing your job. There are no specific formulas to suit all needs and all occasions.

Retirement is a reward for your years of labour. You work for it. You earn it. You are entitled to it.

You should never work for the business; you should make the business work for you.

I have known people who laboured their entire lives so that they could afford a nice house, a car, a yacht, a round-the-world cruise. I also have known people who got so wrapped up in the working that they lost sight of what they were working for.

The sensible business person puts the system to work for him; he does not become a slave to the system.

Retirement provides the opportunity to relieve your mind and body from a lifetime of accumulated tension. You may live longer as a result.

The concept of dying with one's boots on is from a bygone day. It passed along with Custer at Little Big Horn. The few who cling to it today are not doing any service to their businesses, their families, or themselves.

To some, it is a matter of ego to stay on until the bitter end. They would have you — and themselves — believe that they are indispensable. In reality, of course, there are no indispensable human beings — a fact that people would discover if they could remain on earth, ghostlike, for six months after they have passed away.

What is the purpose of achievement if there is no reward for achievement? And what is the reward for doing good work? More work? That isn't a reward; it's a punishment.

Work can become a habit, and habits can be hard to break. Work can become as addictive — and as harmful — as alcohol or narcotics. Keep your life in perspective.

It will help if you can determine what you want to do after you retire. Those who have the most difficulty with retirement are those who have no hobbies, no interests outside their work, no new challenges to confront them. They are the people who were workaholics prior to retirement, and therefore retirement makes them feel like they are going through a period of withdrawal.

The earlier an individual begins to orientate herself to some goal, the more satisfaction she will receive by attaining it. Make retirement one of your goals — and begin planning for it now.

Don't make your retirement decisions alone. Talk to your spouse about it. Talk to your children about it. Plan for it together. Enjoy it together.

Only you can establish the particulars of your retirement. Retire when you're 55. Retire when you have been able to save an estate worth £500,000. Retire when your daughter can prove that she's capable of taking over the business. Retire as soon as you're able to hire somebody to run the business for you. Retire when it's no longer fun to get up in the morning and go to work.

Whatever goal you set, prepare yourself for it. And when that day finally arrives, go ahead and do it!

WHO ELSE MUST BE HAPPY?

A large part of success comes from self-satisfaction: Satisfaction from doing a good job. Satisfaction from having accomplished something worthwhile. Satisfaction from having received the admiration and respect of your peers.

It is highly unlikely, in our view, that an individual could ever consider himself successful solely on the basis of his title or his annual income or his net worth. These things contribute to one's success, but they are not the only criteria.

As an entrepreneur, you have taken on the responsibility for an extended family of individuals: Your employees. The families of your employees, who rely heavily on you. Your suppliers, and their families. Your customers. Your partners or shareholders, and their families.

The way you conduct yourself and your business has a marked effect on these people. Are you successful in handling that responsibility?

Have you maintained and expanded your personal friendships since you became the head of your own business? Would those friends consider you successful in anything other than economic terms?

Have you maintained and strengthened your relationships with your spouse and the other members of your family? Are you a success from their perspective?

In a national survey, people cited the following factors as their criteria for personal success, from most important to least important in the order shown:

- Good health
- Enjoyable job
- Happy family

- Good education
- Peace of mind
- Good friends
- Intelligence
- Unlimited money
- Talent
- Luck
- Luxury car
- Expensive home

In 1904, a magazine conducted a contest to see who could provide the best definition of success. Mrs. Bessie Anderson won the prize with this: 'He has achieved success who has lived well, laughed often and loved much.' It is a definition that wears well with age.

Appendix 1

CONTACT ADDRESSES
REFERRED TO IN THE TEXT

Accepting Houses Committee
101 Cannon Street,
London EC4N 5BA
Telephone 01-283 7332
(Merchant banks, equity and loan finance)

Association of British Factors
Moor House,
London Wall,
London EC2 5HE
Telephone 01-638 4090
(Debt factoring services)

Association of Certified Accountants
29 Lincoln's Inn Fields,
London WC2A 3EE
Telephone 01-242 6855
(Members are professional accountants)

British Franchise Association
75a Bell Street,
Henley-on-Thames,
Oxon RG9 2BD
Telephone 0491-578049
(Members are established franchisors)

British Coal Enterprise Ltd
14-15 Lower Grosvenor Place
London SW1W 0EX
Telephone 01-630 5304
(Finance, advice and training for firms in coal closure areas)

British Venture Capital Association
24 Upper Brook Street,
London W1Y 1PD
Telephone 01-836 5702
(Members offer venture capital — loans and equity)

BSC (Industry) Ltd
Ground Floor
Canterbury House,
2-6 Sydenham Road,
Croydon CR9 2LJ
Telephone 01-686 2311
(Finance, advice, training and workshops in steel closure areas)

Business in the Community (BIC)
227a City Road,
London EC1V 1LX
Telephone 01-253 3716
(Umbrella organization for Local Enterprise Agencies)

Chartered Institute of Patent Agents
Staple Inn Building
High Holborn,
London WC1V 7PZ

Companies Registration Office
55-61 City Road,
London EC1Y 1BB
Telephone 01-253 9393

Companies Registration Office
Exchequer Chambers
102 George Street
Edinburgh EH2 3DJ
Telephone 031-225 5774

Companies Registration Office
Crown Way,
Maidny,
Cardiff CF4 3UZ
Telephone 0222-388588

Co-operative Development Agency
Broadmead House
21 Panton Street,
London SW1Y 4DR
Telephone 01-839 2987
(Headquarters, will provide local contacts)

Dun and Bradstreet
26-32 Clifton Street
London EC2P 2LY
(Company information)

Ethnic Minority Small Business Centre
Queens College
1 Park Drive,
Glasgow G3 6LP
Telephone 041-334 8141

Finance Houses Association
18 Upper Grosvenor Street,
London W1X 9PB
Telephone 01-491 2783
(Members offer hire purchase and other short term finance)

Highlands and Islands Development Board
Bridge House,
27 Bank Street,
Inverness, IV1 1QR
Telephone 0463-234171
(Finance, information, and advice)

Institute of Chartered Accountants in England and Wales
Chartered Accountants Hall
PO Box 433,
Moorgate Place,
London EC2P 2BJ
Telephone 01-628 7060

Institute of Chartered Accountants in Scotland
27 Queen Street,
Edinburgh, EH2 1LA
Telephone 031-225 5673

Institute of Management Consultants
5th Floor,
32-3 Hatton Garden,
London EC1N 8DL

ICC Information Group Ltd
16-26 Banner Street
London EC1Y 8QE
(Company information)

Jordan's Business Information Service
Jordans House
47 Brunswick Place
London N1 6EE
Telephone 01-253 3030
(Company information)

Livewire
c/o Peter Westgarth
60 Grainger Street
Newcastle Upon Tyne NE1 5JG
Telephone 091-261 7856
(Finance and advice for under 25s)

The Local Enterprise Development Unit
Lamont House,
Purdy's Lane
Belfast BT8 4TB
Telephone 0232-491031
(Finance, information, and advice)

Local Investment Networking Company (LINC)
4 Snow Hill,
London EC1A 2DL
Telephone 01-236 5702
(Contacts with investors)

Northern Consultants Association
Unit 1a,
Mountjoy Research Centre
Durham City DH1 3SW
Telephone 091-386 0800
(Lists a wide range of consultants)

The Patent Office
States House,
66-71 High Holborn
London WC1R 4TP
(Patents, trade marks, service marks and registered designs)

Prince's Youth Business Trust
8 Jockey's Field,
London WC1R 4TJ
Telephone 01-430 0521
(Finance and advice for under 25s)

Project Fullemploy
102 Park Village East,
London NW1 3SP
Telephone 01-387 1222
(Finance and advice for young people)

Rural Development Commission
141 Castle Street
Salisbury,
Wiltshire SP1 3TP
Telephone 0722-336255
(Finance, business and technical advice)

Scottish Development Agency
Small Business Division
Rosebery House,
Haymarket Terrace,
Edinburgh EH12 5EZ
Telephone 031-337 9595
(Finance, information and advice)

Venture Capital Report
The Refuge Building,
20 Baldwin Street,
Bristol BS1 1SE
Telephone 0272-272250
(Publishes investment propositions)

Welsh Development Agency
Treforest Industrial Estate
Pontypridd,
Mid Glamorgan CF37 5UT
Telephone 044-384 1666
(Finance, information and advice)

Women in Enterprise
26 Bond Street,
Wakefield, Yorks WF1 2QP
Telephone 0924-361789
(National network of advice and training for women)

Appendix 2

DEPARTMENT OF TRADE AND INDUSTRY

The DTI provides grants and information services under the following categories:

- Consultancy Initiatives:
  - Marketing
  - Design
  - Quality
  - Manufacturing Systems
  - Business Planning
  - Financial and Information Systems
- Research and Technology Initiative
- Regional Initiative
- Export Initiative
- Business and Education Initiative
- Support Services

Contacts and further information are available from the following regional offices:

North-East
Cleveland, Durham,
Northumberland, Tyne & Wear.
Consultancy Initiatives:
091-235 7292
Other Initiatives: 091-232 4722
Stanegate House
2 Groat Market
Newcastle-upon-Tyne NE1 1YN

North-West (Manchester)
Cheshire (except Chester),
Cumbria, Lancashire, Greater
Manchester and the High Peak
District of Derbyshire.
All initiatives: 061-838 5000
75 Mosley Street
Manchester M2 3HR

North-West (Liverpool)
Liverpool, Widnes/Runcorn,
Wiral/Chester, and St. Helens/
Wigan.
All Initiatives: 051-224 6300
Graeme House
Derby Square
Liverpool L2 7UP

Yorkshire and Humberside
North Yorkshire, South
Yorkshire, West Yorkshire and
Humberside.
Consultancy Initiatives:
Leeds 0532-338 300
Regional Enterprise Grants:
0532-338 360
Other Initiatives: 0532-443 171
Priestley House
3-5 Park Row
Leeds LS1 5LF

East Midlands
Nottinghamshire, Derbyshire
(except the High Peak District),
Leicestershire, Lincolnshire and
Northamptonshire.
Consultancy Initiatives:
Nottingham 0602-596 460
Regional Enterprise Grants:
Northampton 0604-21051
ext 35
Other Initiatives: 0602-506 181
Severns House
20 Middle Pavement
Nottingham NG1 7DW

West Midlands
Formerly West Midlands
Metropolitan County, Hereford
and Worcester, Shropshire,
Staffordshire and
Warwickshire.
All Initiatives: 021-631 6181
Ladywood House
Stephenson Street
Birmingham B2 4DT

South-East (London)
Greater London, Kent, Surrey,
Sussex.
Consultancy Initiatives: 01-627 7800
Other Initiatives: 01-730 9678
Bridge Place
88-89 Eccleston Square
London SW1V 1PT

South-East (Cambridge)
Bedfordshire, Cambridgeshire,
Essex, Hertfordshire, Norfolk,
Suffolk.
All Initiatives:
Cambridge 0223-461 939
The Westbrook Centre
Milton Road
Cambridge CB4 1YG

South-East (Reading)
Berkshire, Buckinghamshire,
Hampshire, Oxfordshire and
Isle of Wight.
All Initiatives: Reading 0734-395 600
40 Caversham Road
Reading
Berkshire

South-West
Avon, Cornwall (including
Isles of Scilly), Devon, Dorset,
Gloucestershire, Somerset and
Wiltshire.
Consultancy Initiatives:
Bristol 0272-308 400
Regional Enterprise Grants:
Penzance 0736-60440
Other Initiatives: 0272-272 666
The Pithay
Bristol BS1 2PB

Scotland: Scottish Office
All Initiatives: 041-248 4774
Industry Department for
Scotland
Alhambra House
Waterloo Street
Glasgow G2 6AT

Wales: Welsh Office
Consultancy Initiatives: 0443-841777
(24 hours) or if you live
in Mid Wales Dial 100 and ask
for **Freefone New Wales.**
Other Initiatives: 0222-823185
(24 hours)
Welsh Office Industry Department
New Crown Building
Cathays Park
Cardiff CF1 3NQ

Appendix 3

DEPARTMENT OF EMPLOYMENT SMALL FIRMS CENTRES AND ENTERPRISE ALLOWANCE SCHEME

The Small Firms Service offers free counselling to business start-ups from experienced businesspeople. In addition they offer business development counselling to existing firms at competitive rates.

The Small Firms Service can be contacted on FREEPHONE ENTERPRISE

The headquarters is:

Small Firms Service
Department of Employment
Steel House,
Tothill Street,
London SW1H 9NF
Telephone 01-213 3000

The addresses of the regional offices are:

Birmingham
Sixth Floor
Ladywood House
Stephenson Street
Birmingham B2 4DT
021-643 3344

Bristol
Fifth Floor
The Pithay
Bristol BS1 2NB
0272-294546

Cambridge
Carlyle House
Carlyle Road
Cambridge CB4 3DN
0223-63312

Cardiff
16 St David's House
Wood Street
Cardiff CF1 1ER
0222-396116

Glasgow
120 Bothwell Street
Glasgow
G2 6TU
041-248 6014

Nottingham
Severns House
20 Middle Pavement
Nottingham NG1 7DW
0602-581205

Leeds
1 Park Row
City Square
Leeds LS1 5NR
0532-445151

Liverpool
Graeme House
Derby Square
Liverpool L3 9HJ
051-236 5756

London
Ebury Bridge House
2-18 Ebury Bridge Road
London SW1W 8QD
01-730 8451

Manchester
Third Floor
320-325 Royal Exchange
Buildings
St Ann's Square
Manchester M2 7AH
061-832 5282

Newcastle
Centro House
3 Cloth Street
Newcastle upon Tyne NE1
3EE
0632-325353

Reading
Abbey Hall
Abbey Square
Reading RG1 3BE
0734-591733

DEPARTMENT OF EMPLOYMENT ENTERPRISE ALLOWANCE SCHEME

The scheme provides a grant of £40 per week for one year to people who are unemployed and start a business. Details can be obtained from your local Jobcentre.

Appendix 4

THE TRAINING AGENCY AND TRAINING AND ENTERPRISE COUNCILS

The Department of Employment's Training Agency and the industry-run Training and Enterprise Councils sponsor a wide range of training courses. These include programmes for self-employment, start-up, growth, exporting, management and technical skill development. Start-up training is currently free.

Grants which cover about half the cost of approved training may be available to small firms. This training is often linked to consultancy on business development.

For further information contact the local Area Office of the Training Agency (formerly the Manpower Services Commission), your local Training and Enterprise Council (TEC) or the local Training Access Point (TAP).

If you are unable to locate the address of your local office then contact the Head Office of the Training Agency at the address below.

Department of Employment
The Training Agency
Moorfoot
Sheffield
S1 4PG

Telephone 0742-753275

Appendix 5

PUBLIC LIBRARIES OFFERING PATENT AND BUSINESS INFORMATION

Aberdeen
Commercial Department
Central Library
Rosemount Viaduct
Aberdeen
AB9 1G1   0224-634622

Aberystwyth
National Library of Wales
Aberystwyth
Dyfed
SY23 3BU   0970-3816

Belfast
Commercial Department
Belfast Public Libraries
Royal Avenue
Belfast
BT1 1EA   0232-243233

Birmingham
Patent Department
Central Library
Chamberlain Square
Birmingham
B3 3HQ   021-235 4537

Bradford
Commercial Department
Central Library
Prince's Way,
Bradford, West Yorkshire
BD1 1NN   0274-753656

Bristol
Commercial Department
Central Library
College Green
Bristol
BS1 5TL   0272-276121

Coventry
Reference Department
Central Library
Bayley Lane
Coventry
CV1 5RG   0203-25555

Edinburgh
Reference Department
Central Library
George IV Bridge
Edinburgh
EH1 1EG   031-225 5584

Glasgow
Science and Technology Dept
Mitchell Library
North Street
Glasgow
G3 7DN   041-221 7030

Huddersfield
Reference Library
Kirklees Public Libraries
Princess Alexandra Walk
Huddersfield, West Yorkshire
HD1 2SU   0484-513808

Hull
Technical Library
Central Library
Albion Street
Hull
HU1 3TF   0482-224040

Leeds
Patents Information Unit
32 York Road
Leeds
LS9 8TD   0532-488747

Leicester
Information Service
Central Library
Bishop Street
Leicester
LE1 6AA   0533-556699

Liverpool
Patent Department
Central Library
William Brown Street
Liverpool
L3 8EW   051-207 2147

London
Science Reference Library
25 Southampton Buildings
Chancery Lane, London
WC2A 1AW   01-405 8721

London
Science Museum Library
South Kensington
London
SW7 5NH   01-589 3456

Manchester
Patents Department
Central Library
St. Peters Square
Manchester
M2 5PD   061-236-9422

Middlesbrough
Reference Department
Central Library
Victoria Square
Middlesbrough
TS1 2AY   0642-248155

Newcastle-upon-Tyne
Commercial Department
Central Library
Princess Square
Newcastle-upon-Tyne
NE99 1MC   0632-617339

Norwich
Reference Department
Central Library
Bethel Street
Norwich
NR2 1NJ   0603-61127

Nottingham
Business Department
County Library
Angel Row
Nottingham
NG1 6HP   0602-412121

Plymouth
Reference Department
Central Libary
Drake Circus
Plymouth
PL4 8AL   0752-264675

Pontypridd
Library
Polytechnic of Wales
Pontypridd
Mid Glamorgan
CF37 1DL 0443-405133

Preston
Reference and Information
Service
Harris Library
Market Square
Preston
PR1 2PP 0772-53191

Swindon
Reference Department
Divisional Library
Regent Circus
Swindon
SN1 1QG 0793-27211

Portsmouth
Reference Department
Central Library
Guildhall Square
Portsmouth
PO1 2DX 0705-819311

Sheffield
Commerce & Technology
Department
Central Library
Surrey Street
Sheffield
S1 1XZ 0742-734742

Wolverhampton
Reference Department
Central Library
Snow Hill
Wolverhampton
WV1 3AX 0902-773824

Appendix 6

A SELECTION OF USEFUL ADDITIONAL READING

Getting Ideas

Which Business? by Stephen Halliday (Kogan Page 1987)

Earning Money at Home edited by Edith Rudinger (Consumers Association 1987)

Starting up

The Greatest Little Business Book by Peter Hingston (Hingston 1987)

Lloyds Bank Small Business Guide by Sara Williams (Penguin Books 1987)

Sources of Information

The Small Business Guide by Colin Barrow (BBC Publications 1984)

Where to find Business Information. Business In the Community (1988)

Raising Finance

Raising Finance; The Guardian Guide for the Small Business by Clive Woodcock (Kogan Page 1985)

Venture Capital and the Growing Business by Peat, Marwick, Mitchell and Co. (1985)

Index